Patchwork Souvenirs
of the
1933 World's Fair

1. CENTURY OF PROGRESS
combined with WORLD WITHOUT END

Maker: Aurora See Dyer
Chicago, Illinois, 1933

Pieced and appliquéd: 87″ x 70″; cotton

Collection of the Dyer Family Trust.

Patchwork Souvenirs

of the

1933 World's Fair

MERIKAY WALDVOGEL
BARBARA BRACKMAN

RUTLEDGE HILL PRESS
Nashville, Tennessee

Published in Nashville, Tennessee, by Rutledge Hill Press, 211 Seventh Avenue North, Nashville, Tennessee 37219. Distributed in Canada by H. B. Fenn and Company, Ltd., Mississauga, Ontario.

Typography: D&T/Bailey Typography, Inc., Nashville, Tennessee
Design and Jacket: Harriette Bateman
Art: Tonya Pitkin Presley, Studio III Productions

Library of Congress Cataloging-in-Publication Data

Waldvogel, Merikay, 1947–
Patchwork souvenirs of the 1933 Chicago World's Fair / Merikay Waldvogel, Barbara Brackman.
p. cm.
Includes bibliographical references and index.
ISBN 1-55853-257-9
1. Quilting—Competitions—Illinois—Chicago—Exhibitions. 2. Patchwork quilts—United States—History—20th century—Exhibitions. 3. Century of Progress International Exposition (1933–1934 : Chicago, Ill.) I. Brackman, Barbara. II. Title.
TT835.W337 1193
746.9'7'097307477311—dc20 93-22421
CIP

Manufactured in Hong Kong through Palace Press
2 3 4 5 6 7 8 — 98 97 96 95 94

The Exhibition
Patchwork Souvenirs of the 1933 World's Fair
curated by
Merikay Waldvogel and Barbara Brackman
is developed and coordinated by
the Knoxville Museum of Art and
Smith-Kramer, Incorporated,
with funding support from
The American International Quilting Association

For our mothers

Helen Tasa Waldvogel
Cecelia McNally Brackman

Who never knew what we became,
who never made quilts
but taught us to finish what we started.
They would be very proud.

CONTENTS

ILLUSTRATIONS

Owners of Illustrated Quilts

Eleanor Alford
Maxine Armstrong
Birmingham Museum of Art
Carl Carpenter
Chicago Historical Society
Evelyn Crittenden
Lois Hobgood Crowell
Norma Darling
Robert Dyer
Marilyn Forbes
Evelyn Galbraith
Artie Fultz Davis
Joyce Gross
Amy Hoyt
Mary Hurst
Ardis and Robert James
Shirley Jillson
Phin and Lucille Kinnaman
Sharon Kline
Sue and Thorne Longsworth
Marjorie Malone
Margaret McDonald and Charles Fitzgerald
Lora Lee Parrott
Kathryn Tate Putnam
Evelyn and Clarence C. Rebenstorff
Anna Reiser and Alice Katzmareck
Susan Salser
Ada Schlick
Stearns Technical Textiles Company
Susan Smith
Marilyn Woodin
Shelly Zegart

1933 Sears National Quilt Contest Chronology

January 1933	Sears National Quilt Contest announced
May 15, 1933	Sears quilt contest deadline
May 18, 1933	Judging of local contests
May 20–23, 1933	Exhibits of local quilt contest entries Winners sent on to ten regional contests
May 25, 1933	Judging of regional contests
May 28, 1933	1933 Century of Progress Exposition opens
June 1–6, 1933	Exhibits of quilts in regional contests Top three winners in each region sent on to final round of judging
June 8, 1933	Judging of thirty finalists
June 15, 1933	Exhibit opens at Sears Pavilion on fair site
August–October, 1934	Exhibit of ten regional first prize winners repeated

PREFACE

The 1933 World's Fair was a press agent's carnival. To divert Depression-weary newspaper readers, Hollywood starlets were ready to expose a leg or two in front of any and all exhibits. Details of the India-to-Chicago trek of a dedicated Hindu fairgoer were flashed around the country. On a dull day at the fair, there was always a contest, one to discover the person with the most freckles, another to crown the Healthiest Boy and Girl. There was a Husband Calling Contest, and Mary Pickford chose the Sixteen Happiest Married Couples in the United States. (Six months later she filed for divorce from Douglas Fairbanks.) Sears, Roebuck and Company, the supplier of the American dream, chose to sponsor a contest for the Best Quiltmaker in the country.

Sixty years later the freckles have faded and undoubtedly some of the happy marriages went the way of Mary and Doug's, but the quilts inspired by the Sears contest have endured, and with them the story of their making—splendid and unusual souvenirs from the 1933 fair.

The Sears National Quilt Contest stands as one of the most important events in American quiltmaking history because in a short period of time it encouraged the making of tens of thousands of quilts by women vying for the grand prize of $1,200 and the honor of having their quilts on public display. Quilt contests have been organized since, but none has been as successful in attracting so many entries.

When I was writing *Soft Covers for Hard Times: Quiltmaking and the Great Depression,* I included a chapter on the 1933 Sears National Quilt Contest since it had an important impact on the number and kind of quilts made during the 1930s. Barbara Brackman, Joyce Gross, and Cuesta Benberry had already reported on the contest—its structure, judges, prizes, and so forth.[1] I decided to see how the contest worked in the Southeast.

In my research, I came upon 1933 newspaper accounts and even photos of the winning quilts. I also heard the story of the grand prize-winning quilt entered by a woman from Lexington, Kentucky, who had not actually made it. The daughter of the woman who had pieced the quilt was ready to tell me her mother's story, and she had the cloth pieces to prove it. Barbara had heard a similar story from the daughter of another woman who had also worked on it. Other quilt historians had suspected as much, but no one had been able to prove the allegation.

What surprised me most was that of the 25,000 quilts entered in the contest, only fifty or sixty had been located by the mid-1980s. Barbara thought many would surface during the state quilt surveys. Some quilts with contest entry tags or green merit ribbons still attached were easy to identify. Descendants of the contest's quiltmakers sometimes contacted Barbara with stories about Sears quilts. Occasionally, a quiltmaker herself, such as Inez Ward of Horse Cave, Kentucky, told about the excitement of winning a prize in the contest.

Then the quilts carrying pictorial messages exalting the Century of Progress began to appear in antique auction notices and magazines. With their unusual modern appliqué motifs such as buildings, airplanes, and zeppelins, these quilts were easily identified as Sears Quilt Contest entries. Barbara compiled information on all these quilts in her computer.

After my book was published, she and I decided to collaborate on an in-depth book and exhibit of quilts entered in the Sears Quilt Contest. We both felt we had just scratched the surface of this story. Thousands of quilts were entered in the contest, and we had seen only a handful. Newspapers, we knew, carried detailed accounts of the local and regional contests, but only a few clippings had been found. Although we had the list of the thirty finalists showing their hometowns, which had been published in the 1934 Sears catalog, information about most of the winners was not now easily accessible. With a combined, concerted effort, we felt that we might be able to track down more of the quilts and their makers.

Especially intriguing to us was the story of the making of the grand prize-winning quilt and the fact that it had disappeared after Mrs. Roosevelt received it. Finding that missing quilt would bring us the grand prize for quilt sleuthing.

We embarked on an adventure of locating more prize-winning quilts by scanning microfilm of newspapers and conducting interviews with the quiltmakers' descendants. Fortunately, some of the winners had kept all the correspondence concerning their quilts—the application form, the congratulatory letters from Sears, and even letters from companies asking for their testimonials about quilting supplies used in their prize-winning quilts. This information served as a valuable resource for piecing the story together.

We also placed requests for information about Sears contest quilts in newspapers, museum magazines, and quilt history publications. As each of us gave lectures, we asked the audience for leads.

In 1992 we traveled to eastern Kentucky to find information on the six Kentucky quilts that reached the final round of judging. One of the six was the grand prize winner made by Margaret Rogers Caden of Lexington, Kentucky. We interviewed sixteen people in two days. The quiltmakers' relatives and friends welcomed us with smiles and open photo albums. The information enlightened us as to the extent of professional quilting in Kentucky during the 1920s and 1930s, and we began to understand how the grand prize-winning quilt was made—with several experts performing different tasks but working separately on the same quilt. Unfortunately, we did not find the quilt itself, but some of the women had saved leftover or practice pieces of the quilt, which we photographed for inclusion in this book. Also the Stearns and Foster Company has agreed to lend a replica of the quilt made years after the fair from a pattern featured on their Mountain Mist batting wrapper.

As we finish this book, we continue to gather information about Sears Contest quilts. We have identified 123 quilts. Of the final round of 30 winners, we have identified 21 and located 10. Six of the finalists have been lent to the exhibit which accompanies this book. We also have studied 54 commemorative quilts, but we know more exist. Sears archivists have saved photos of missing quilts, including the grand prize winner. State quilt projects have recorded some Century of Progress quilts. Occasionally, 1933 World's Fair quilts appear in auction brochures. In the appendix of this book, we have included lists of Sears Contest winners in several local and regional contests. We encourage our readers to look for accounts in their local newspapers between May 20 and June 15, 1933, and then try to find the quiltmaker or her descendants.

Today's historiographers emphasize the importance of placing material culture (such as quilts) and oral history (such as quilt stories) in the context of when they were produced. In this case, we felt it was important to study not only the contest, but also Sears, Roebuck and Company, the Century of Progress Exposition of 1933, the history of Chicago, and the theme of the fair—the blending of science and technology.

Chicago, known for its "I Will" spirit, planned the fair to celebrate the city's one hundredth birthday. Sears, headquartered in Chicago, joined in the celebration by building its own corporate pavilion on the fair site. The

2. Aurora See Dyer, 1960

Aurora See Dyer (1895–1969)

In 1933 Aurora Dyer was president of the Cook County Women's Christian Temperance Union. The organization planned a booth at the fair. With her club work and the making of her Sears Contest quilt, the family anticipated the opening of the fair with enthusiasm.

Her son Robert remembers the making of the quilt. His mother had a frame set up in a second floor bedroom. "We never got dinner that spring," he joked about her determination to win the contest. The colors are an unusual combination, but she was going for the "modern" look.

The quilt won a green ribbon of honorable mention award at a Chicago store contest.

3. CLIPPER SHIP

Maker: Unknown
Possibly made in Michigan, 1933

Appliqué and embroidery: 81″ x 76″; cotton

Sea gulls swirl, reminding viewers of the distances explorers have traveled. From Spain on a Clipper Ship, across the Atlantic on a plane, to America's West in covered wagons, all roads in 1933 led to Chicago's World's Fair represented by the Sears exhibition hall.

Collection of Shirley Jillson.

idea for a national quilt contest, which originated in the advertising department at Sears, turned out to be a public relations coup as 25,000 quilts were entered and newspapers clamored to report the results.

The most elaborate quilts in design and quilting techniques emerged as winners in local and regional rounds of the Sears National Contest. If these quilts, reflecting the epitome of quiltmaking standards at the time, had been the only type quilt entered, the contest might have passed unnoticed. Instead, its organizers decided to add a special category for quilts of "original designs" commemorating the theme "Century of Progress." Sears added a bonus prize of two hundred dollars if a Century of Progress quilt was judged the grand prize winner. Unfortunately, only two theme quilts reached the final round.

In choosing the quilts in this book and the accompanying exhibit, we attempted to include as many of the quilts judged in the final round as possible, because these quilts are evidence of the high standards of quiltmaking at the time. However, we felt the commemorative quilts, overlooked by the contest judges, deserved attention at long last since these one-of-a-kind creations provide insight into the makers' views of the profound technological changes from 1833 to 1933. We also have included quilts made from patterns produced after the fair to illustrate the contest's impact on quiltmaking.

Behind each quilt is the story of the maker and her family. Quiltmakers remember the excitement of the quest for the $1,200 prize and the pressure to meet the contest deadline. Quiltmaking during those four months in 1933 was surely fast and furious. We heard stories of husbands helping to draft the patterns, of children having to fend for themselves at dinner time since Mother was quilting, and of one quiltmaker whose early May attack of hay fever sent her to bed unable to finish her masterpiece. Through these human interest stories, we view life during the 1930s from a perspective heretofore unrecorded.

The twisting plot of the 1933 Sears National Quilt Contest has a cast of intriguing characters, all sure their quilts will bring them fame, glory, and much-needed extra change in their pocketbooks. Played out against the bleak landscape of the Great Depression, the contest quickly comes to a close with a not-so-happy ending at the Rainbow City's tribute to a Century of Progress.

Barbara Brackman began researching the contest in the late 1970s when she was a resident of Chicago. Hundreds of people have responded to her requests for information about contest quilts.

4. Mayme Heltman Barnfield, 1930s

Mayme Heltman Barnfield (1875–1945)

With several years of art education prior to her marriage, Mayme Barnfield knew color and design. Since originality was to be important in judging, she created her own design. Unfortunately, she became ill with a severe case of hay fever and was unable to finish the quilt on time. In the fall of 1933, the family moved to Oklahoma where the quilt was finished.

We wish to thank Joyce Gross, Cuesta Benberry, and Wilene Smith for sharing their research and vast files of ephemera on the 1933 National Quilt Contest. Lenore Swoiskin and Vicki Cwiok at the Sears Archives in Chicago answered questions about the contest and referred many quilt owners to the authors. The Sears archives provided black-and-white photographs of the various stages of the contest.

After the quilts were chosen for the book, the authors set out to secure more information about them and their makers' lives. Each quilt in this book carries with it a story of the search for the current owners. Luckily for the authors, owners were enthusiastic about helping to find photographs and information to add human interest to the quilt. Our volunteer sleuths included H. M. Carpenter, Carol Fichtner, Floyd and John Leonhard, Norma Darling, Margaret McDonald, Bryding Henley of the Birmingham Museum of Art, Carter Houk of *Ladies Circle Patchwork Quilts,* Ruth Anderson, Mary Jo Richardson, Margie Sexton, Helen Truett, Susan Salser, Karen Finn, Evelyn Galbraith, Robert Klemenz, Riverside California Municipal Museum, and Julie Silber.

State quilt documentation project officers combed their records for 1933 Sears Contest quilts. We especially wish to thank the New York Quilt Project, the Heritage Quilt Project of New Jersey, Michigan Quilt Project, Texas Quilt Project, the Minnesota Quilt Project, West Virginia

5. GARDEN KALEIDOSCOPES

Maker: Mayme Heltman Barnfield
Illinois, 1933

Pieced: 86″ x 73″; cotton

Collection of Amy Barnfield Hoyt, daughter

Heritage Quilt Search, the Indiana Quilt Registry Project, and the Illinois Quilt Research Project.

Several quilts not in the book required the help of many people. We wish to thank those people for their efforts: Jean Loken, Fawn Valentine, Roberta Farmer, Jean Long, Barbara Kilbourn, Helen Bentley, Joann Woodward, JoAnn Pecenka, Marie Salazar, Marguerite Wiebusch, Betty Bell, Peggy Potts, Amy C. Turner, Sherri Hughes, Karey Bresenhan, Ruth Homuth, Erma Schmidt, Dorothy Cozart, Bets Ramsey, Laurel Horton, Pat Nickols, Vista Mahan, Winifred Reddall, Mary Alma Parker, Sandra G. Munsey, Marilyn Goldman, Phyllis Tepper, Terry Broder, Nancy Tsupros, Creta Lindenmuth, Cora Kanupkie, Hazel Carter, Allene Helgeson, Avis Kriebel, Margaret Maxwell, LaVerne Larson, Mary Girvin, Sally Pundt, and Carol Waldvogel.

The souvenirs featured in the book and the exhibit are from the collections of Norma Darling, Steve Waldvogel, and the authors. William and Katharine Brehm provided a videotape of home movies taken at the 1933 World's Fair.

Our Kentucky expedition included many interviews with descendants and friends of the famous quiltmakers from the mountains of Kentucky. We thank them for inviting us in and telling us their family stories: Helen Black, Elberta Botner, Ruth Stewart, Louise Eddleman, Sarah Caden, Robert and Mary Klemenz, Sally W. Smith, Reva Crabtree, Bertha Hensley, and Anna Marshall of the Owsley County Senior Citizens.

For their work in the planning of the exhibit, we thank the staff at the Knoxville Museum of Art, especially curators Stephen Wicks, Joyce Gralak, and Leslie Tate-Boles.

David Smith and his staff at Smith-Kramer Fine Arts have promoted the traveling exhibit and now have secured museum sites for all twelve venues.

Quilting buddies in Knoxville—Linda Claussen, Becky Harriss, Susan Stephens, and Sheila Rauen—helped with the quilt photography sessions at the studio of Gary Heatherly, whose work presents these quilts in a glorious light. Doug Smiley skillfully produced precise copies of black-and-white photographs and did it with a smile and door-to-door service.

Without the owners of the quilts included in this book, the story of the 1933 Quilt Contest might not have been shared with new generations of quilt enthusiasts. We thank them for trusting us with their quilts and family stories.

We also thank all the participating museums: Society of the Four Arts in Palm Beach, Florida; Museum of Our National Heritage in Lexington, Massachusetts; Midland County Historical Society in Midland, Michigan; Dane G. Hansen Memorial Museum in Logan, Kansas; the Chicago Historical Society; Edsel and Eleanor Ford House in Grosse Point Shores, Michigan; Gene Autry Western Heritage Museum in Los Angeles, California; the Rock County Historical Society in Janesville, Wisconsin; the Bergstrom Mahler Museum in Neenah, Wisconsin; and the University Art Museum of the University of Kentucky in Lexington.

Without libraries, this book would never have come to life. We thank the Knox County Public Library, Knox County Archives, University of Tennessee Library, Chicago Public Library, the University Library at the University of Illinois at Chicago, Louisville Free Public Library, Lexington Public Library, University of Kentucky Library-Department of Special Collections and Archives, and the Lee County (Kentucky) Public Library.

Museums shared quilts, photographs, and printed materials. We wish to thank Anita Jones, associate textile curator at the Baltimore Museum of Art; Robert Goler, curator of decorative arts at the Chicago Historical Society; and Bryding Henley at the Birmingham Museum of Art.

Finally, we want to acknowledge the support of the American Quilt Study Group, founded in 1980 by Sally Garoutte, of Mill Valley, California. Today the organization based in San Francisco boasts an international membership of more than 700 quilt researchers and enthusiasts. By providing a vehicle through its seminars and journal *Uncoverings,* the group serves as a network to disseminate and collect information about quilts and quilt events. Without such an organization, the history of the 1933 National Quilt Contest might not have resurfaced in the 1990s.

Patchwork Souvenirs

of the

1933 World's Fair

The Rainbow City

Chicago and the Fair

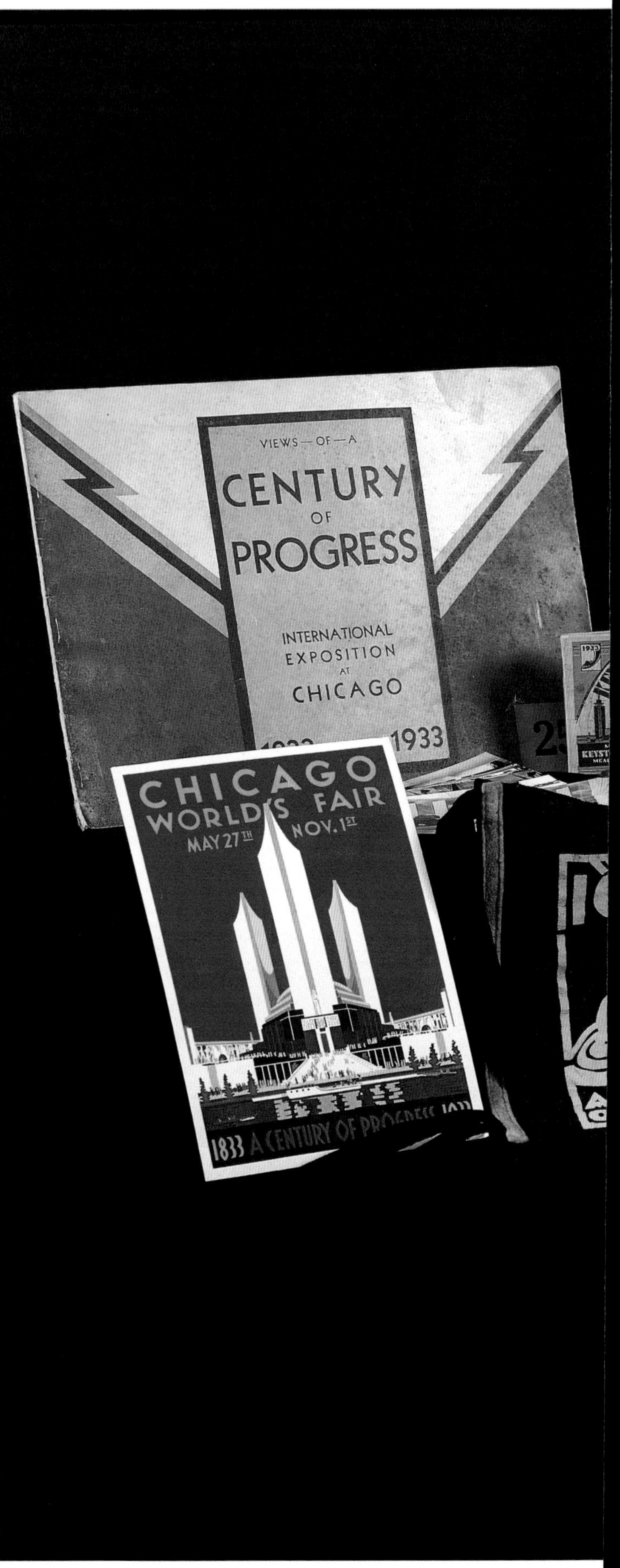

6. Souvenirs of the Chicago World's Fair of 1933. Collection of Barbara Brackman.

Chicago's 1933 World's Fair came to be known as the Rainbow City because of its brightly colored modern buildings, just one of the many contrasts with its earlier world's fair in 1893, the World's Columbian Exposition dubbed the Great White City, with its classic white buildings bathed in the light of thousands of incandescent bulbs at night.

Although the fairs differed in size, architecture, and long-term effects, they also had their similarities. Both fairs were intended to tout Chicago's accomplishments, put it center stage among world cities, generate income, and stimulate investment in further development. Unfortunately, both fairs faced difficult financial times as they occurred during two of the worst economic periods in American history.

1893 Chicago World's Fair

In the early 1890s, the U.S. Congress accepted bids from New York City, Washington, D.C., St. Louis, and Chicago to commemorate "Columbus's voyage." Chicago sent a delegation of civic leaders who boasted about their city's transportation services, cultural attractions, climate, available land, and funding. This bragging earned Chicago its nickname, the Windy City.[1]

East Coast leaders looked down on the upstart sixty-year-old city out in the scruffy midsection of the nation. They questioned whether Chicago would find the funding to mount an exposition on a scale like the great European

DIMENSION
STEREOSCOPE
Photographers
CHICAGO SOUVENIR GUIDE TO A CENTURY OF PROGRESS
OFFICIAL VIEW BOOK
A CENTURY OF PROGRESS EXPOSITION
No. 1A POSTAGE 1½c WITHOUT MESSAGE
CHICAGO
GMC
Greyhound Lines
1934

7. Woman's Building at the 1893 World's Columbian Exposition with Ferris wheel in the background. Courtesy of Chicago Historical Society. Photograph ICHi-16265 by Harrison.

expositions. Who, they wondered, would trek to the Midwest just to see a fair? However, backers of the Chicago fair had organized early and by 1890 had financial pledges of $10 million. In the end, "it was the money that talked," and the U.S. Congress voted to give the determined Chicagoans a chance to prove themselves.

Chicagoans knew they could do it. They had proved to themselves they could overcome great odds when they rebuilt their city following the fire of 1871. They were proud of the city's population growth from 550 in 1833 to 350,000 in 1893. They wanted to show to the world what they could do. That fierce determination to overcome all odds became the official city motto: I Will.

Frederick Law Olmsted, a noted landscape architect, drew a site plan for the World's Columbian Exposition on a 700-acre undeveloped piece of land in Jackson Park on the city's South Side bordering Lake Michigan. The fair planners proposed a classical design for the buildings, and nationally known architects, many of whom were from the East, designed the massive exhibit halls with colonnades and statuary on terraces, pools, and lagoons. The buildings were white and no outdoor signs were allowed, so the fair became known as the White City.

The exhibit halls surrounding the large formal basin known as the Court of Honor included the Mines and Mining Building, the Electricity Building, the Machinery Building, and the mammoth Manufactures and Liberal Arts Building that covered thirty acres. At one end on a huge pedestal stood a colossal gold statue of a woman symbolizing the Republic. The overall effect was one of symmetry, beauty, and grandeur.

8. Olive Thomas Wetzel, 1902

Olive Thomas Wetzel (1877–1964)

The family of Olive Thomas Wetzel's mother were early settlers and wealthy landowners in St. Clair County in southern Illinois. Her father, Edward L. Thomas, an engineer and lawyer, made and lost fortunes speculating in coal mines and railroads. He sent his daughters to the private Mary Institute school in St. Louis. Olive later attended Vassar College but returned home to nurse her mother through a terminal illness.

In 1914 Olive and her sister moved in with her brother who was a well-known and politically active county highway superintendent. The spinster sisters had an active social life as officers in church societies and the Daughters of the American Revolution. At this time, Olive developed a quiet friendship with William Wetzel, who worked for her brother as a handyman.

Two days after her sister's death, Olive eloped with William. They moved fifty miles away to a remote farm community. For the next forty-one years, she lived happily in a house without indoor plumbing or central heating tending her garden and raising chickens. She continued to live on the farm years after her husband died.

Her nieces fondly remember Olive wearing colorful dresses made of feed and flour sack cloth and telling stories of the family foibles and eccentricities.

9. STATE OF ILLINOIS

Maker: Olive Thomas Wetzel
Nashville, Illinois, 1933

Pieced: 82″ x 66″; cotton

Collection of Mary Hurst, niece

Buildings outside the Court of Honor included the Palace of Fine Arts, the Woman's Building with exhibits of women's work and demonstration cooking lessons in a model kitchen, the Children's Building with child care services, the Horticulture Building, and the only colorful exhibit hall, the Transportation Building designed by Chicago architect Louis Sullivan, which contained large railroad displays.

Free noon concerts of classical music further enhanced the feeling of heaven on earth. However, the common man was more attracted to the music of John Philip Sousa at the area outside the Court of Honor. The Midway with its signature structure, the Ferris wheel, became the most popular gathering place. At night the fairgrounds burst into brilliance as its white buildings were illuminated with thousands of electric light bulbs.

From May through November 1893, the fair attracted 27.5 million visitors. Then the great white buildings were destroyed, but their classic architectural forms affected both public and private building designs for decades to come.

Taking little time to bask in the success of the 1893 exposition, a team of architects led by Daniel H. Burnham drew up an ambitious city plan with extensive public parks, broad avenues, and commercial sectors. The city faithfully followed the plan as industries and businesses established home offices there. The great skyscrapers went up; city parks, schools, the train system, and expanded cultural facilities helped Chicago gain a reputation as a city worth visiting. This growth continued strong into the early twentieth century.

Chicago's First One Hundred Years

As Chicago approached its one-hundredth birthday in 1933, city leaders were eager to host another World's Fair. Its population had grown to 3.5 million, ten times the population in 1893. The 1933 Century of Progress Exposition would celebrate one hundred years of Chicago history.

10. Detail of Fort Dearborn Quilt by Mary Fitzgerald (number 127, page 85)

11. Detail of Fort Dearborn Quilt by Mary Fitzgerald (number 127, page 85)

Before the coming of European explorers, Indian tribes including the Potawatomi, Menominee, and Shawnee used "Checagou," a swampy area along the shores of Lake Michigan where many trails crossed, as a meeting place. Explorers Father Marquette and Louis Joliet arrived in 1673, and others followed to settle there because of the area's proximity to the Mississippi River. A short portage to the Illinois River gave access to the great river system of the midcontinent.

First France, then Great Britain, and finally the United States controlled the area around Chicago. In 1803 the U.S. government established Fort Dearborn. Skirmishes with hostile tribes occurred frequently, but the most memorable was in 1812 when the Indians killed all the inhabitants and burned Fort Dearborn. It was the first of many hardships the people of Chicago had to overcome. White Americans established their present dominance in 1816 when Fort Dearborn was rebuilt and the Indians were relocated to Indian Territory in the present-day states of Kansas, Nebraska, and Oklahoma.

In 1830 the town was surveyed, and the following year Cook County was organized with Chicago as its county seat. In 1833, the settlement of 550 people was incorporated. Four years later the population had grown to 4,000. A canal was built in 1848 to eliminate the portage to the Illinois River. As the city grew, services were added, including a water works system in 1833, street lighting in

12. 1871 Chicago Fire in appliqué on I Will Quilt (number 121, page 82)

1850, and railway connections in the 1850s. During the 1860 Republican convention held in Chicago, the city achieved national recognition when Illinois resident Abraham Lincoln was nominated for president. In that year the city's population was over 109,000 and by 1870 it had grown to 306,000.

In 1871 a small fire, spreading rapidly through the city of frame houses lining wooden streets, destroyed 17,500 buildings valued at $196 million, and leveled one-third of the city. About 300 people died, and 90,000 were left homeless.[2] The Chicagoans' "I Will" spirit had never known such a challenge, but by 1880 the damage was repaired and Chicago ranked fourth in population among American cities.

After the fire, some of the city's best-known cultural attractions were established, the Chicago Public Library in 1872, the Art Institute of Chicago in 1879, and the Chicago Symphony Orchestra in 1890. Then came the World's Columbian Exposition held in the summer of 1893.

1933 Chicago World's Fair

To celebrate Chicago's one-hundredth birthday, Chicago architect Edward H. Bennett envisioned a fair that would be twice as large as the greatest expositions of the time. Architects and engineers throughout the country submitted plans for fabulous structures, such as a "three-mile-high" mountain of exhibits on Lake Michigan with an elevator to carry fair-goers to the top; a $3 million steel observation tower more than twice as tall as the Eiffel Tower; and a monumental Tower of Water and Light rising high out of a lagoon.[3]

Critics of the fair believed that the advent of radio, moving pictures, and the automobile had made people more traveled, more sophisticated, and less easily thrilled by grandiose expositions.[4] Therefore a proposal for a second Chicago World's Fair was rejected in 1926, but it was revived in 1927.[5]

Lenox Lohr, general manager of A Century of Progress, believed that "A fair must first of all provide high entertainment value. In addition, however, it should have spiritual, patriotic, technical, cultural and educational values, so that the visitor may leave with a sense of . . . personal uplift."[6]

In searching for a theme with general appeal that would also celebrate the centennial of Chicago's birth, the fair organizers proposed various ideas, including the service of science to humanity. This idea caught the attention of officers of the National Research Council, a prestigious organization dedicated to promoting scientific research. With it as a sponsor, the backers of the fair knew that support from other organizations would soon follow.

The theme A Century of Progress, with its emphasis on the progress of the physical sciences and their application to industry, closely paralleled the one hundred years of the city of Chicago. Beginning with the steam locomotive and ending with Lindbergh's solo flight across the Atlantic Ocean, the century from 1833 to 1933 had witnessed profound changes in economic and cultural life brought on by a dazzling number of scientific discoveries.

With the theme decided and enthusiasm growing, the backers of the fair turned their attention to funding. The late 1920s were prosperous times in the United States, so the backers sought private rather than public support. Sale of Founder and Sustaining memberships, at $1,000 and $50, raised more than $271,000, which was used to run the fair offices in the late 1920s.

A membership campaign targeting the citizens of Chicago sold Booster memberships at five dollars each. In return, members received ten admission tickets to the fair and a certificate of membership. Special efforts were made to reach a large number of community groups including industrial organizations, ethnic groups, and civic clubs. Eventually, 118,773 people were enrolled.[7]

13. NINETEEN HUNDRED THIRTY THREE

Maker: Jeanette Morgan Longsworth
Racine, Ohio, 1933

Pieced: 61″ x 81″; cotton

Collection of Sue and Thorne Longsworth, son

Jeanette Morgan Longsworth (1881–1964)

Jeanette Morgan married John Longsworth, and they settled down to a life of farming in Racine, Ohio. She made many quilts during her life. This one was made especially to capture the attention of judges of the Century of Progress Quilt Contest.

The first large-scale funding plan included selling $10 million worth of gold-guaranteed notes paying 6 percent interest, to mature on October 15, 1935. Unfortunately, the first ones were issued one day after the stock market crash of 1929. During the following months, more than 150 banks closed in the area, public school teachers were paid in scrip, and many Chicagoans became unemployed and homeless, needing clothing and food. Yet the city persisted in the plan to celebrate the glories of its past.

The officers of A Century of Progress believed the economic benefits of the 1933 fair could insulate Chicagoans from the most severe effects of the Depression, as the previous exposition had done during the panic of 1893. The president of the Century of Progress Exposition, Rufus C. Dawes, wrote in May 1931 that "benefits as great [as those following the Chicago World's Fair of 1893] will follow the 1933 Exposition."[8]

The leaders of A Century of Progress Exposition reined in their enthusiasm, proposing a more modest architectural layout and instituting a clever financial management plan. Lenox Lohr came up with the idea of building the exhibit halls one at a time, selling the space, then using the money to construct another hall. With the money raised from the bonds, the Travel and Transport Building

14. Jeanette Morgan Longsworth, circa 1954

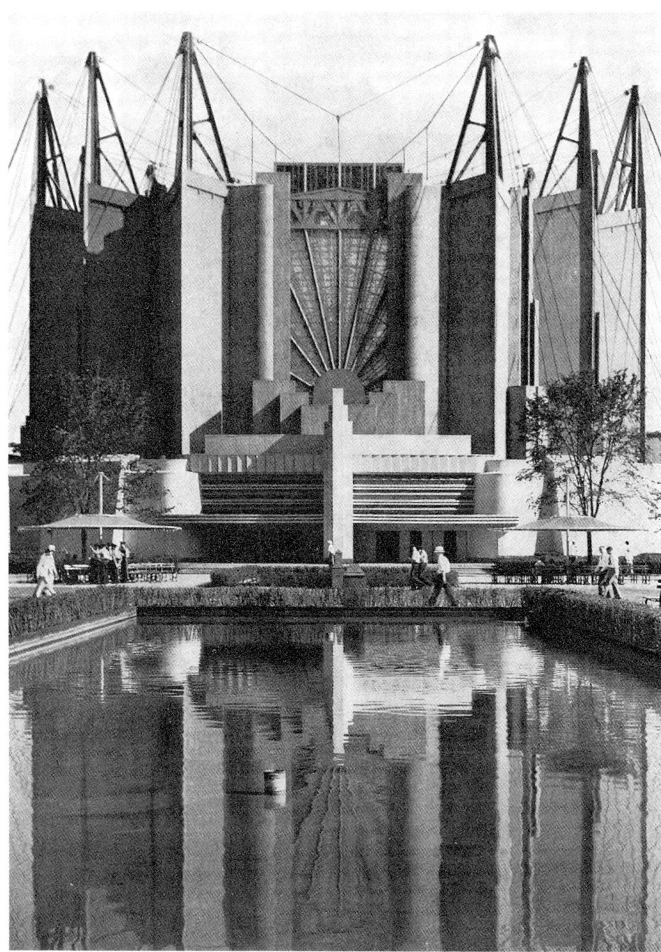

15. The Travel and Transport Building was the first building erected at the 1933 fair site.

was erected. When its space was rented, they erected another building. By the end of 1931, eighteen months before the scheduled opening, six buildings were in place. The cost of exhibit space was ten dollars per square foot. To encourage early payment of the rental fees, A Century of Progress offered a discount, and most exhibitors took advantage of it. Lohr's conservative financial management impressed the local bankers, whose support was vital to fair funding.

Lohr was as good at public relations as he was at fundraising. He encouraged Chicagoans to tour the completed buildings for a small admission fee to heighten interest in the fair. He also invited potential exhibitors to the site, who, after seeing the fabulous buildings and the expansive grounds, often signed contracts.

Working vigorously to lure European exhibitors, Lohr set up an office in Europe and conducted public relations campaigns to counteract Europeans' narrow view of Chicago as the city of Al Capone and his gangsters.[9] He also visited Europe's expositions to discover the latest in exhibitry and building techniques. He was especially intrigued by the animated exhibits and was impressed by

(continued on page 12)

16. To generate excitement, a replica of Fort Dearborn was erected prior to the fair, and Chicagoans could tour the site before the fair opened.

17. CENTURY OF PROGRESS

Maker: Marie Svec Poetz
Chicago, Illinois, 1933

Pieced, appliquéd, and embroidered: 88″ x 66″; cotton

Collection of Norma E. Darling

According to the maker's daughter, Marie Poetz's brother, an electrician at the fair, gave her a book of architectural drawings of the buildings. With the help of the book and several trips to the fair site, Marie Poetz sketched all the buildings and transferred them to cloth, embroidering a record of the fair's main attractions.

The pictures include: the Travel and Transportation Building described as a grand windowless "breathing" building with a suspended roof that expanded and contracted as the temperature varied; the Hall of Science sponsored by the National Research Council featuring a mathematics show and experiments with light rays; the replica of Fort Dearborn, a log reconstruction of the first dwelling at the site of Chicago; the Golden Temple of Jehol, a replica of a temple built on the fair site by Chinese artisans; the Mayan reconstruction of the Nunnery at the ruins at Uxmal on the Yucatan Peninsula of Mexico; and the Sears, Roebuck and Company Building, the only corporate pavilion pictured on the quilt.

18. In outline embroidery the maker included several fair buildings, including the Travel and Transport Building.

19. To depict the lighting of the fair, the maker quilted a light ray emanating from an embroidered star. The ray eventually reaches a point in North America on the globe of the fair logo.

20. Marie Poetz

Marie Svec Poetz (1899–1969)

Marie Poetz was born in Tabor, Czechoslovakia, and came to the United States at the age of three. She was raised in a family of six children on Chicago's South Side. In 1924 she married Henry J. Poetz, a wholesale meat dealer, and lived at 7134 South Claremont Avenue in Chicago. She was a professional seamstress and milliner who also produced all kinds of fancy work. Although she made several quilts, none was like this Century of Progress quilt. She won an Honorable Mention ribbon at one of the six Chicago-area Sears store contests, but it was not shown at the fair.

According to her daughter, Myrl Helwig, "My father told me Mother would sit up working on the quilt until two or four o'clock in the morning. It became an obsession. She kept on until it disrupted her sleep patterns. My father asked her to stop, but she didn't."

Marie Poetz often told the story of seeing the grand prize-winning quilt with her own eyes. "It was so ordinary. Someone with a pattern and a little talent could have made it. If I had known what type quilt the judges would choose, I would not have gone to the trouble I did with my original design. I thought they were looking for something that was unique—a souvenir of the Chicago World's Fair. In the end, the quilt was just an ordinary pattern—something to duplicate easily."

(continued from page 9)

buildings made of plaster of paris on wire. "More economical than permanent stone buildings, and just as effective visually," he cabled his colleagues in Chicago.[10]

By 1932, one year before the planned opening, both time and money were running short, but the fair had sold $3 million of space to exhibitors, and corporations had contributed $2.5 million for construction of their exhibit halls. Because of the Depression, labor and material costs had dropped significantly and developers' dollars went a long way.[11]

One of the immediate effects of the fair was the displacement of people living in shacks along the shores of Lake Michigan in the area where the fair buildings were to be constructed. Martha S. McGrew, first assistant to the fair's general manager, recalls, "It was often heartbreaking, but we had to remember that what we were being paid to do was build a fair, not look after every unfortunate."[12]

On the other hand, the construction on and development of the 424 acres of fairgrounds meant hiring hundreds of out-of-work contractors and laborers. To prepare for the event, the fair had employed 5,500 people.[13]

On opening day, Saturday, May 27, 1933, most visitors were oblivious to the behind-the-scenes juggling of money. Many were feeling better about the future after President Franklin Delano Roosevelt's inaugural address in March. The fair also served as a refuge from the worst of the Great Depression. Once visitors entered the gates, they were transported to a magical world where worries and cares vanished. One *New York Times* reporter describing the feeling at the fair wrote, "The gang's all here, seeking ideas and inspiration, getting back its optimism, reminding its soul that mankind and this proud nation get up and dust off their knees after every tumble and march on toward the glorious future."[14] The first week's attendance of 514,514 far surpassed the first week's attendance of 224,492 at the 1893 fair.[15]

In keeping with their public relations genius, fair organizers organized a scientific triumph to open the exposition. At 9:15 P.M. on the night before opening day, light rays from the star Arcturus entered the eye of the nation's largest telescopes, which magnified the beam and transferred it to a photo-electric cell or "electric eye" that converted the light into electrical impulses. These were amplified many times and transmitted by wire to Chicago to throw the switch that turned on the giant searchlight on top of the Hall of Science.

As the great beam swept across the electric eye on each building, lights illuminated its exterior and interior.[16] With a push of the button, the fair linked Chicago's past success to the city's modern world, as if to say, "You have done it again!"

Arcturus was selected because the rays of light which left the star in 1893, when Chicago was celebrating its first World's Fair, arrived in Chicago in 1933.[17] From that night on, light rays from Arcturus, magnified by telescopes and transmitted by wire, illuminated the fair buildings each night. Arcturus became "the star" of the fair. One account in the *World's Fair Weekly* called it

> the most dramatic moment of every exposition day. . . . Several thousand of the visitors may be sitting at tables on the terrace of a restaurant listening to a famous orchestra . . . or they may be strolling through the midway looking for thrills. But as the time draws near for Arcturus to do its stuff, all heads turn toward the tower of the Hall of Science. . . . The moment the circuit is complete, there is a wild howl of exaltation from the big motor generators it sets to work. The searchlight atop the tower now flashes on. . . . The crowds sigh as though suddenly relieved from some tremendous tension. They have the feeling that they have beheld a miracle.[18]

Arcturus spinning toward Earth became the logo of the 1933 World's Fair—never mind the fact that it looked more like a comet than a star.

By day, the fair site on the Lake Michigan shore, extending from Twelfth Street on the north approximately three miles south to Thirty-ninth Street, was alive with

Beam Of Light From Distant Star Will Throw Switch, Opening Chicago's Fair

This drawing shows how light from the distant star Arcturus will be trapped at four observatories and used to turn on the lights at Chicago's world fair. Telescopes will train the beam of starlight on photo-electric cells which will convert the light into electrical impulses. These will be transmitted to Chicago by wire to turn on the exposition's giant searchlight, shown at the upper left, and the searchlight's rays will turn on the lights in the main buildings.

21. From the *Lexington Herald Leader*, Lexington, Kentucky, May 26, 1933.

National Quilting Association 27th Annual Quilt Show

A "Grand" Parade of Quilts in Grand Rapids, Michigan June 20-23, 1996

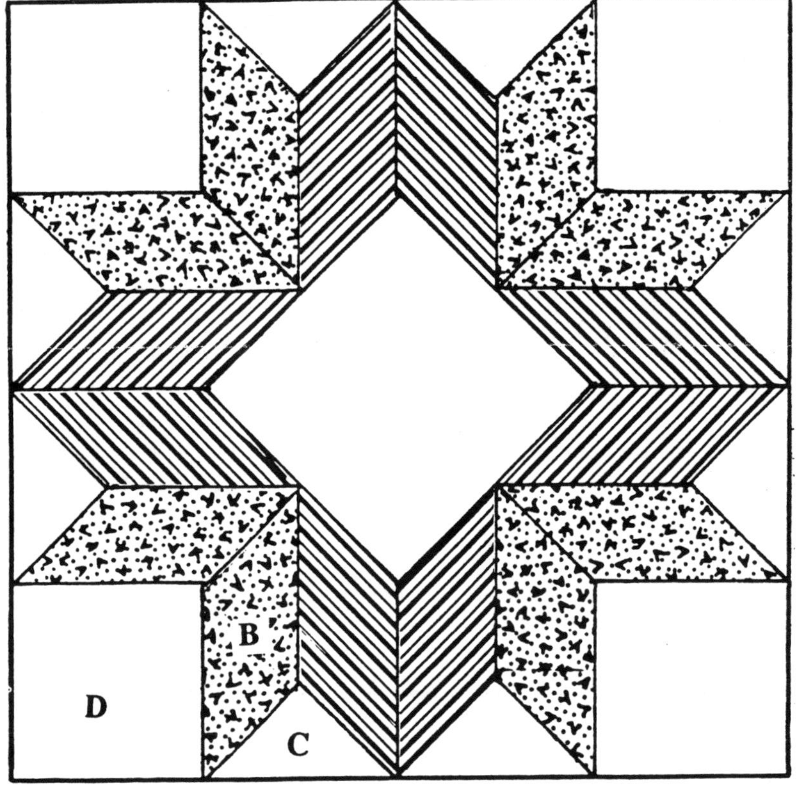

For information send $1.50 to:
(available January 1996)
Brenda Tate
40 Coventry Woods
South Charleston, WV 25309

Michigan Beauty

Pattern for 12-inch block below
4-inch miniature illustration
Add seam allowance
from Practical Needlework Quilt Patterns, Volume III, No. 2 by Clara Stone, ca 1910

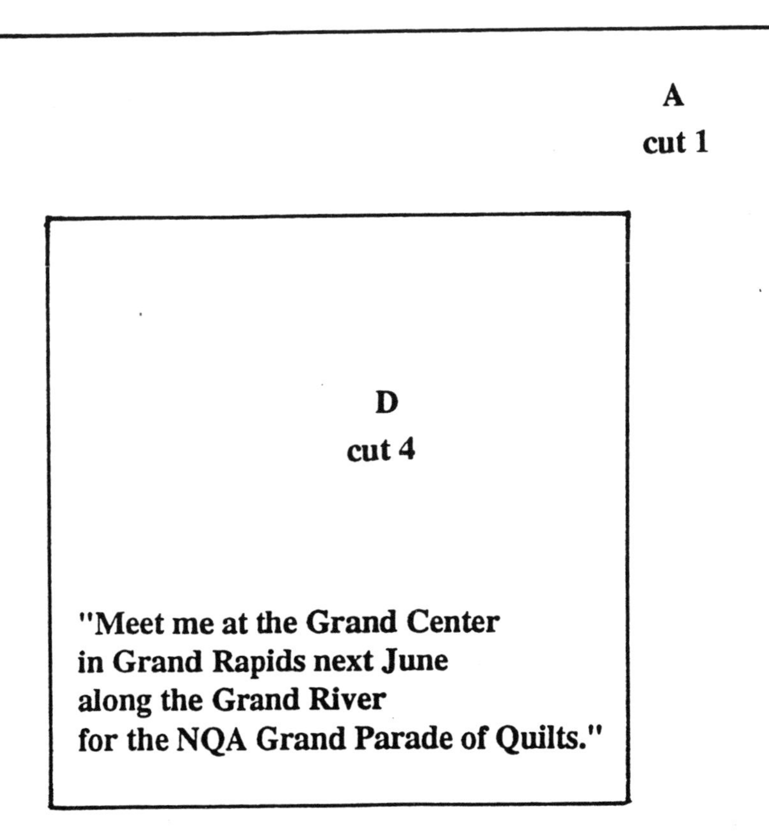

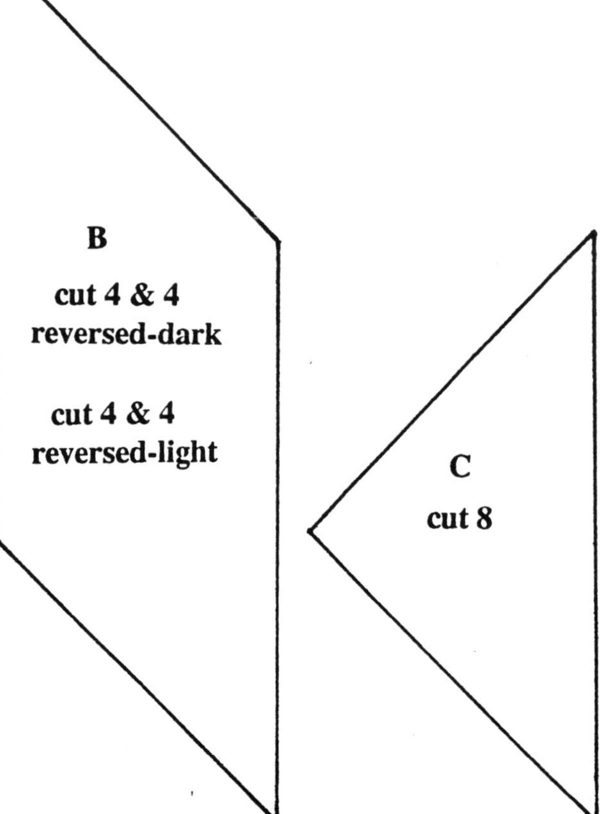

22. Louise Rowley of Chicago chose to feature the fair site on her appliqué quilt. This bird's eye view of the exposition (looking south) contains all the major attractions of the 1933 fair.

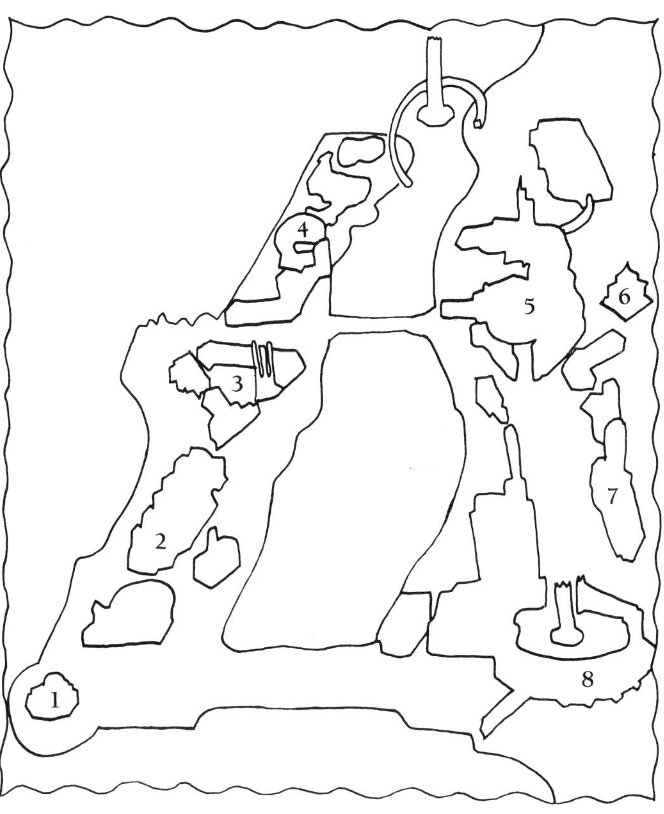

1. Adler Planetarium; 2. Agricultural Building; 3. Federal and States Building; 4. Electrical Building; 5. Hall of Science; 6. Chinese Lama Temple of Jehol; 7. Sears Pavilion; and 8. Administration Building.

activity. On one side the sky and the great blue expanse of the waters of Lake Michigan formed a backdrop to the unusual architectural shapes of the fair's buildings. On the other side was Chicago's famous skyline boasting modernistic skyscrapers. Contrasting sharply with the classical designs seen at the 1893 fair, pavilions of the 1933 fair, with its theme of A Century of Progress, were buildings of the future, radical in construction and design. Most walls were windowless and without ornamentation, and angular towers soared aloft. What shocked most visitors, though, was the color scheme the architects had chosen to unite the disparate forms and angles.

While the 1893 World's Columbian Exposition had been praised as the Great White City, the 1933 A Century of Progress Exposition glowed as the Rainbow City. Lohr explained proudly the reasoning behind the choice of colors. "[Color] gave life to materials not inherently attractive and provided the bright setting and fiesta spirit so essential to a world's fair."[19]

Artist Joseph Urban was responsible for the general color scheme of the site structures. His palette consisted of twenty-three colors, all of the brightest intensity. He chose colors for a particular building to emphasize its unique form. Some structures were painted with color that reflected sunlight by day or searchlights by night in distinctive ways. The psychological effects of certain colors were also taken into account, with inviting reds used at entrances and green with its calming effects at rest areas.[20] In spite of Urban's great plan, many critics found the colors garish, harsh, and uninviting. When the fair reopened for its second summer, the buildings were repainted with the number of colors reduced to ten.

At night, artificial lighting added to the excitement of entering the Rainbow City. While the 1893 World's Columbian Exposition had dazzled the world with the white brilliance of its electrical display, the 1933 A Century of Progress Exposition introduced the gaseous tube or neon. Colorful tubing highlighted the architectural features, and floodlights intensified the buildings' colorful shapes and forms. Low mushroom-shaped lights lined the pathways producing an inviting pool of light.[21]

Other attractions at the fair included the auto assembly line at the General Motors Building; the House of Tomorrow with an all-electric kitchen and central air condition-

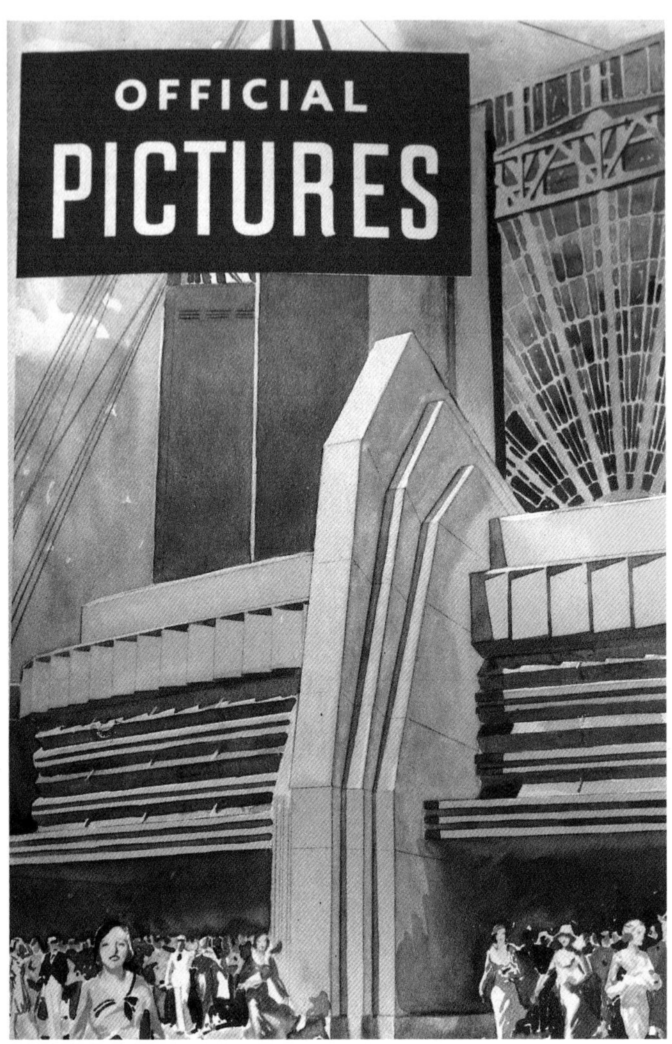

23. Brightly colored buildings gave the 1933 fair the name the Rainbow City. *Official Pictures of the Century of Progress Exposition.* Photos by Kaufmann and Fabry Company. Collection of Steve Waldvogel.

ing; the Electricity Hall where a strange and wonderful invention called television vied for attention with radio; and the Hall of Science, whose exhibits drew thirty times as many visitors as any concession on the Midway.[22]

The U.S. Building included exhibits from all departments of the federal government, including an FBI demonstration of fingerprinting. Adjacent to it was the States' Building in which every state in the union had been offered exhibit space. In spite of the Depression, thirty-two states found the funding to erect exhibits promoting their progress, tourist attractions, and quality of life. The fair also set aside certain days to honor the people and the accomplishments of participating states.

The international presence at the fair softened the hard-edged technological exhibits and enabled Americans to celebrate their multicultural origins. Tucked along the lake shore, the streets of Paris and Belgian, oriental, Moroccan, and Chinese villages welcomed visitors with song, dance, and good food. Streets of Paris became a favorite night spot. Set up to look like a Parisian street corner, with lovely women lounging in doorways and make-believe gendarmes standing guard, the area featured the most famous fair celebrity, Sally Rand, who tantalized the audience with her fan dances.

Some of the more bizarre exhibits included George Washington's false teeth; a cross section of a city dump depicting archaeologically the progress of society from hoop skirts and bustles of the 1870s to contemporary cast-off trappings; Roads of the World, a quarter-mile track that included the Grand Caravan Route, Daniel Boone's Wilderness Road, and imperial roads of China and Rome. The Havoline Tower made in the shape of a giant thermometer was a tribute to Chicago's climate.

The Midway included rides, games of chance, food booths, and side shows such as the Old Plantation Show and circus acts which cost only a few cents. Overhead the pylons of the Sky Ride towered 628 feet high and 1,850

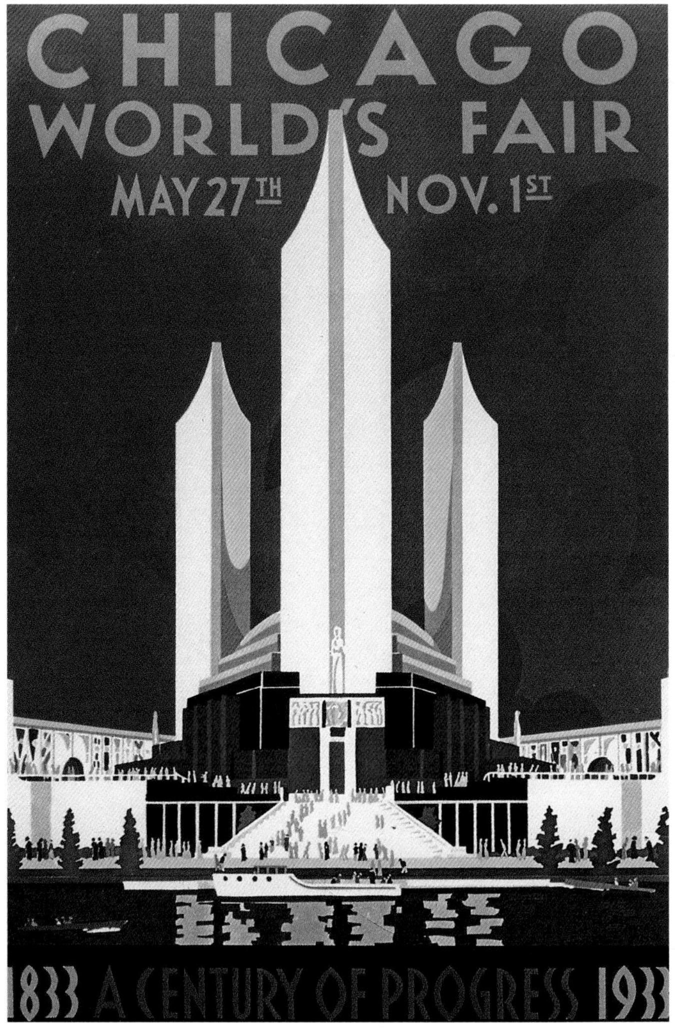

24. Postcard of 1933 Century of Progress poster. Designed by Weimar Pursell.

feet apart. Stretched between the towers were cables on which rocket-shaped cars traveled at a height of 219 feet. Each car had a seating capacity of thirty-six passengers.[23] The Sky Ride was to A Century of Progress what the Eiffel Tower had been to the Paris fair of 1889 and the Ferris wheel to the World's Columbian Exposition of 1893. One of the most popular features of the fair, with 12 percent of the patrons taking the ride, it served as the dominant feature of the fair.[24]

The Art Institute of Chicago organized an exhibit of fine paintings. Bands and orchestras, providing a wide variety of music daily, included the U.S. Marine Band, a one-hundred-piece marimba band, and the Chicago Symphony Orchestra. John Philip Sousa composed "The Century of Progress March" especially for the fair.[25] A pageant of transportation called "Wings of a Century" was performed daily by 150 actors with horses, full-size trains, automobiles, a clipper ship, and a model of the Wright Brothers' first airplane.[26]

26. Murals showing a century of progress in General Electric exhibit in the Electric Hall.

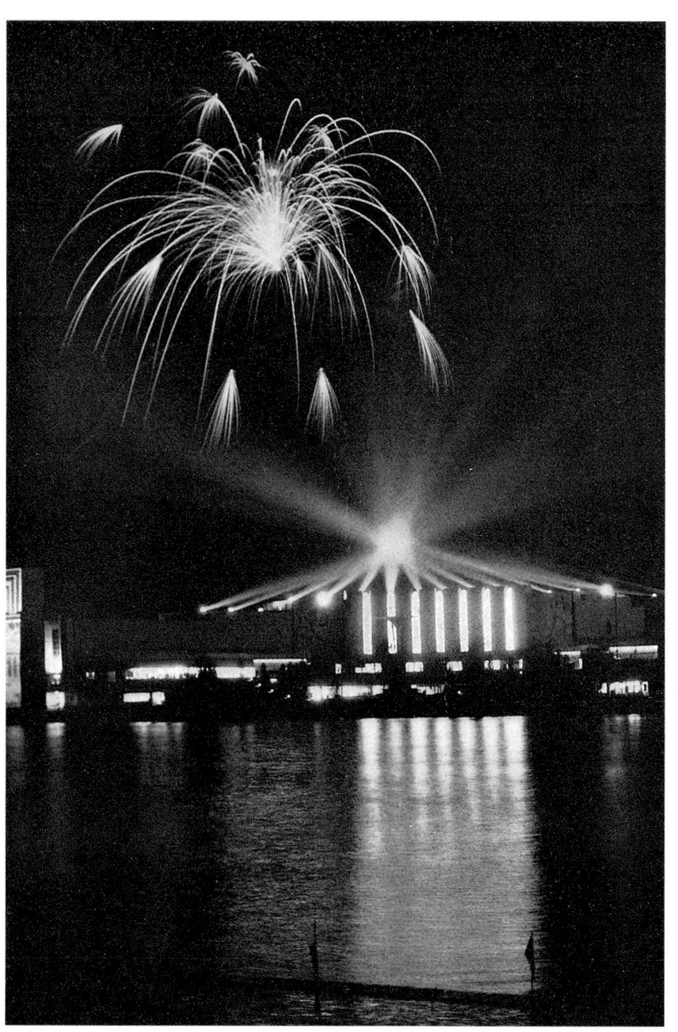

25. The Electrical Building—Illumination and Fireworks.

27. Café de la Rotonde—Streets of Paris.

28. Post card of one of the most unusual buildings at the fair—the Havoline Thermometer.

29. Looking south on the Midway.

30. At Enchanted Isle parents left their children for supervised activities.

31. College students earned extra money as tour guides pulling roller chairs.

With all these attractions spread over a three-mile-long site often under an intense summer sun, fair-goers sought refuge in cool, quiet areas such as the Horticultural Gardens or reception areas in exhibition halls. Others rented roller chairs driven by young male athletes recruited from nearby universities. The chairs cost the rider one dollar per hour, with the driver keeping thirty cents. Most drivers provided a guided tour, hoping for a large tip.[27]

A popular spot for weary parents who needed free time was The Enchanted Isle, sponsored by the Junior League of Chicago. Proclaimed "the world's largest playground for children," the supervised area was a child's dreamland, including rides such as small-scale trains, planes, and automobiles to drive.

The Sears Pavilion, one of the largest corporate buildings at the fair, served as a registration center providing rest rooms, free checking facilities, telephones, and telegraph offices. The building contained a huge relief map of the United States and a loudspeaker system that told the story of Sears's distribution network from factories and warehouses to mail-order centers and retail stores. Wall dioramas traced the history of merchandising in the one hundred years from 1833 to 1933.[28]

Outside the building, visitors sat on the verandas overlooking the fair site, enjoying a light meal and rest. Inside, Sears held daily demonstrations, such as how to modernize a kitchen and how to wash and dress a baby properly. A woodworking shop with the best tools attracted thousands of interested hobbyists.[29] Among the attractions was the exhibit of thirty regional prize-winning quilts on display from mid-June through the end of the fair.

On November 1, 1933, the fair was scheduled to end. Later general manager Lohr would write:

> The Fair had attracted more people than any previous celebration, the exhibitors were well satisfied, most concessions had been profitable . . . and the City of Chicago had benefited by the millions of [new dollars] that had been transfused into its financial arteries. Yet there was no popular demand for a continuation for the simple reason that since it had never been done, it was not considered possible.[30]

The sudden decision to reopen the fair was made a few weeks before the scheduled closure for one main reason: insufficient funds to pay the bonds in full. Lohr felt a deep moral obligation to fulfill that promise.

To attract visitors to the fair in 1934, the organizers knew they had to overcome the perception that it would be "the same old fair." A nationwide publicity campaign began in January 1934, encouraging those who had missed the fair to come the following summer. The Midway was moved to another site to make room for an increased number of foreign villages, a very popular feature of the 1933 fair. Two outdoor theaters were constructed, including one where the daily Arcturus ceremony was continued. Ford Motor Company constructed an entirely new $3 million building. Transportation was improved, and numerous new restaurants were opened. Probably the most appreciated innovation was free toilets.

The fair closed for good in the fall of 1934. Sally Rand remembered the last day, November 11:

> Mass hysteria took over. They completely demolished the Century of Progress. They tore down flags, they tore down street lights, they tore down the walls. It started out being souvenir hunters, but it became mass vandalism. Anybody who witnessed it had this terribly frightening feeling.[31]

The 1934 fair was as successful as its predecessor, according to Lohr, attracting more than sixteen million paying customers. Most importantly, the bonds were paid in full, and a surplus of $160,000 was divided among the Chicago Park District, the Museum of Science and Industry, the Art Institute, the Adler Planetarium, and other institutions. In the months that followed, demolition crews cleared the site of all but a few buildings. Today only the Shedd Aquarium and the Adler Planetarium remain. Many of the exhibits were donated to Chicago's Museum of Science and Industry.

The fair accomplished its goal of raising the image of Chicago in the eyes of the nation. The city once again overcame great odds to produce a world-class celebration of scientific triumph and technological progress. And for a few glorious months in the summers of 1933 and 1934, the fair turned the nation's attention from the Great Depression at home and the war brewing overseas.

32. SEARS PAVILION

Maker: Lora McKinley Montgomery
Fort Wayne, Indiana, 1933

Appliqué: 77½″ x 66″; cotton

Collection of Lora Lee Parrott, daughter.

33. Lora McKinley Montgomery, 1935

34. The Sears, Roebuck, and Company Pavilion.

Lora McKinley Montgomery (1896–1989)

Lora McKinley was raised in Temple, Texas, married a minister, and in 1933 had three small children at home. Lora Montgomery saw a picture of the proposed Sears exhibit hall and asked an artist to draw it to scale for the size of her quilt. Finding enough shades of gray in fine cotton material was the next difficult step. She chose to quilt zeppelins, biplanes, and a train in the large plain areas behind the central motif. Neighbors visited often to see the progress of her quilt. She told her family the three elderly gentlemen judging the Fort Wayne quilts only liked "yellow flowers on quilts."

A Century of Progress in Quiltmaking

The Quilting Context

The 1920s were a period of economic prosperity and lively cultural life. Americans had extra income to purchase automobiles, decorate their homes, and buy the latest fashions. They hoped the memories of the Great War would disappear quickly in the euphoria of prosperity. In 1920, city dwellers outnumbered those living in the rural areas, and urban areas began to expand rapidly.

At the same time, Americans expressed a concern for preserving and celebrating the country's historic and cultural past. Quilts and other Early American antiques such as furniture, ceramics, silver, and paintings were revered, duplicated, and preserved. Community leaders launched programs to save historic homes and villages, such as Colonial Williamsburg.

Millions of immigrants had entered the United States in the early 1900s bringing with them their distinctive cultural values and traditions. African-Americans were moving into mainstream society and up the social ladder. Women were exerting their political influence and by 1920 had won the right to vote. Americans of northern European descent worried about the loss of the "American" identity. Editors, who sensed a fear of the future and a nostalgia for a rosy past, published stories, poetry, and pictures pointing out the irony of the modern age: although fast-paced urban life was exciting, true American values resided in the rural areas and in the preservation of traditional crafts. Advertising romanticized the Puritan

35. Detail of Vases of Flowers (number 47, page 30)

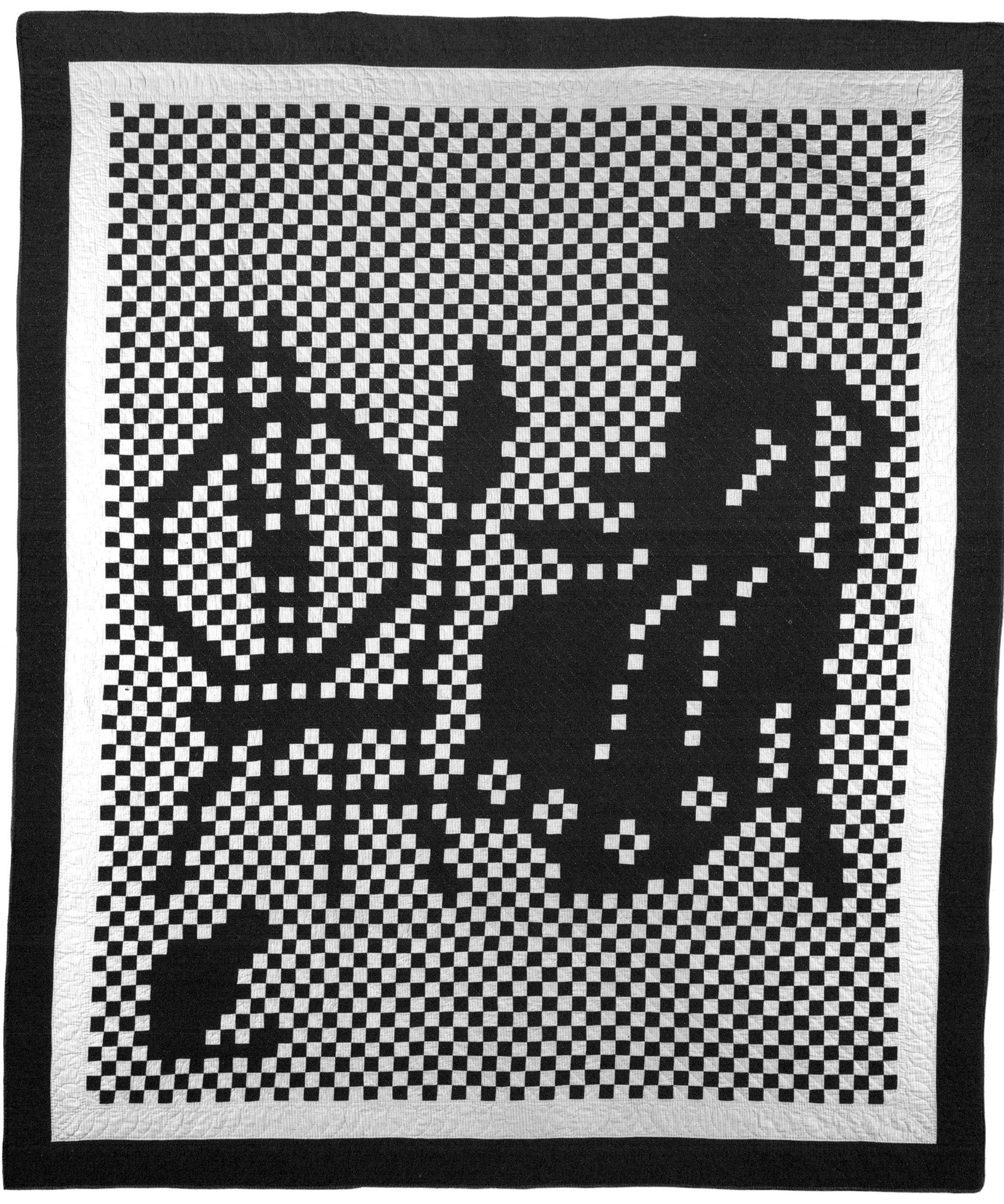

36. LADY AT THE SPINNING WHEEL

Maker: Emma Andres
Prescott, Arizona, 1933

Pieced: 82″ x 70″; cotton

Collection of Joyce Gross.

37. Emma Andres. Courtesy of Joyce Gross.

Emma Andres (1908–1987)

Emma Andres spent her entire life in Prescott, Arizona. By reading magazines and newspapers for sale in her father's cigar store, she discovered the world outside Prescott. When she sent to a women's magazine for an appliqué quilt kit, it marked the beginning of a lifetime interest in quiltmaking and quiltmakers. Through a newspaper article, she discovered Charles Pratt, a quiltmaker famous for pictorial quilts made of tiny squares of colored silk. For years they maintained a friendship through letters. This quilt, with 3,630 pieces, simulates Pratt's quilt designs.

Emma Andres developed lifelong friendships with quiltmakers such as Florence Peto and Carrie Hall. She proudly displayed scrapbooks of correspondence from these famous quilters along with her own prize-winning quilts in her Happiness Museum, the name she gave to her father's store when she became the owner.

work ethic with its emphasis on resourcefulness, hard work, and pride in a job well done.

A quilt conjured up images of the colonial homemaker sitting beside the fire in a rocking chair. With her work done and her children in bed, the homemaker filled her free time with a worthy activity. In 1928, a writer for *Southern Agriculturalist* described such a scene: "Picture the cozy wood fire in the long winter evenings, with the women of the family gathered around the light cutting and sewing bright bits, pink, red, white and yellow."[1]

The quilt became a patriotic emblem, an object of immense cultural value. Historical quilts and other textiles served as a tangible link to the past. Poet Doris Wheeler Blount wrote, "If you want to steal away from the strife of the modern age to thoughts of bygone days, lay it over your lap, this emblem of a vanished past—a magic carpet gay—great-grandma's coverlet."

The message of the Colonial Revival appealed to women of the 1920s, even the "modern" ones dressed in their flapper dresses and cloche hats who lived in homes with steam heating and indoor plumbing. Quilt designers encouraged the new woman to "give it a try." Magazines and newspapers provided patterns for sophisticated quilt designs in the latest colors to match the urban decorating taste of the 1920s. Businesses enticed novice quiltmakers with new timesaving methods and tools.

Marie Daugherty Webster of Marion, Indiana, is credited with spearheading the quilt revival of the early twentieth century. After she created sophisticated quilts for her family using her own patterns based on floral images, her friends encouraged her to send one of her quilts to the *Ladies Home Journal,* whose editor, Edward Bok, was eager to promote new ideas in decorating and crafts. When her innovative quilts appeared in 1911 and 1912 in the magazine, she became an overnight quilt authority. She and her family members produced patterns for her quilts and sold them by mail order. In 1915, Doubleday Book Company asked her to write a book that would appeal to the quiltmaker as well as to the quilt collector. *Quilts, Their Story and How to Make Them* became an important source of quilt history. Webster traced the roots of quiltmaking, researched quilts in private and museum collections, and provided a list of quilt pattern names. By the end of the year, the book was in its second printing.

38. Marie Daugherty Webster (1859–1956) of Marion, Indiana

39. MAGPIE ROSE

Maker: Euphemia Medona Anderson Mounts (1864–1953)
Carlinville, Illinois, 1933

Appliqué: 87″ x 76″; cotton

The appliqué pattern was designed and sold by Marie Webster, whose mail-order company sold patterns from Marion, Indiana.

Collection of Ardis and Robert James.

40. MAY GARDEN

Maker: Etelka Geisler Galbraith
Hinsdale, Illinois, 1933

Pieced: 91″ x 78″; cotton

Although strongly influenced by design changes advocated by quilt designers Marie Webster and Anne Orr, Etelka Galbraith created her own appliqué design for this quilt.

Collection of Evelyn Galbraith, daughter-in-law.

41. Etelka Galbraith with her husband, Ralph, in Loose Park Rose Garden in Kansas City in 1947.

Etelka Geisler Galbraith (1888–1986)

Throughout her lifetime Etelka Galbraith made fifty-five quilts and kept records and working sketches for most of them. Besides making quilts, she researched the origins of quilting and other handwork. Her notebooks contain accounts of visits to museum textile collections to see quilts discussed in books by Marie Webster and Ruth Finley. In the mid-1930s, she gave lectures to Chicago women's clubs and often illustrated them with quilts from her own collection. In 1936, she presented a program entitled "Quilts" on a Chicago radio station.

"Mrs. Galbraith's program is both historical and practical, tracing the history of quiltmaking from older days to the present time. Her own display of quilts and manner of presentation add much to the hours of enjoyment. I am happy to recommend her charming personality, and splendid program for Women's Clubs."—Mrs. Frank Staely, Illinois Federation of Women's Clubs.

Webster's work had a major impact on the color, style, and construction of quilts in the twentieth century. She preferred soft, pastel, plain fabrics to printed ones. She advocated a return to the appliqué quilt style with a central medallion surrounded by borders. Most importantly, she opened the door to new ideas evolving from long-standing quiltmaking traditions. A distinctly new American quilt was born. Through her patterns and her writing, she revived quiltmaking and led the way for thousands of quiltmakers and quilt historians who followed.

Other women's magazines, eager to match the offerings of *Ladies Home Journal,* sought quilt designers and writers to add to their staffs. *Good Housekeeping* originally employed Anne Orr as a needlework designer to write a regular column on knitting, crochet, cross-stitch, and tatting, but in 1921, as the quiltmaking revival was gaining strength, Orr offered her first appliqué quilt pattern in the magazine.

Through the 1920s and early 1930s, magazines and newspapers increased their attention to quilt patterns. Stearns and Foster Company, the quilt batting manufacturers, estimated in 1934 that at least 400 metropolitan newspapers were regularly publishing information on quiltmaking. A Gallup survey in six large cities showed that the quilt article was the most popular Sunday feature, with 32 percent of the women reading it.[2]

A few periodicals carried an exclusive quiltmaking feature. One was the *Kansas City Star,* in which fashion editor Edna Marie Dunn supervised patterns mailed in by readers. Most newspapers published syndicated columns, with Ruby Short McKim one of the earliest columnists. Her patterns for embroidered blocks appeared before 1920. In 1929 she began drawing patchwork designs for papers across the country.

The Nancy Page Quilt Club was another popular feature. Florence LaGanke Harris, a food writer for the *Cleveland Press,* entertained readers with the fictional account of Nancy's weekly Tuesday club meeting. Regular members Martha, Charlotte, and Dorothy discussed the pattern of the week with Nancy who lectured about its history, construction, and suggested color schemes. Nancy Cabot was the pseudonym for a columnist at the *Chicago Tribune* who began her daily pattern feature in January 1933, possibly in response to Sears's announcement of the World's Fair contest. Loretta Leitner Rising, who had earlier edited a column in which readers confessed to their most embarrassing moments, provided approximately 2,000 patterns during the 1930s.

42. IRIS

Maker: Flora Sexton Wade
Knoxville, Tennessee, 1933

Appliqué: 89″ x 75″; cotton

Flora Wade's quilt won second prize in the Atlanta regional contest and was shown at the 1933 Chicago World's Fair.

Collection of Kathryn Tate Putnam, grandniece.

43. Detail of Iris

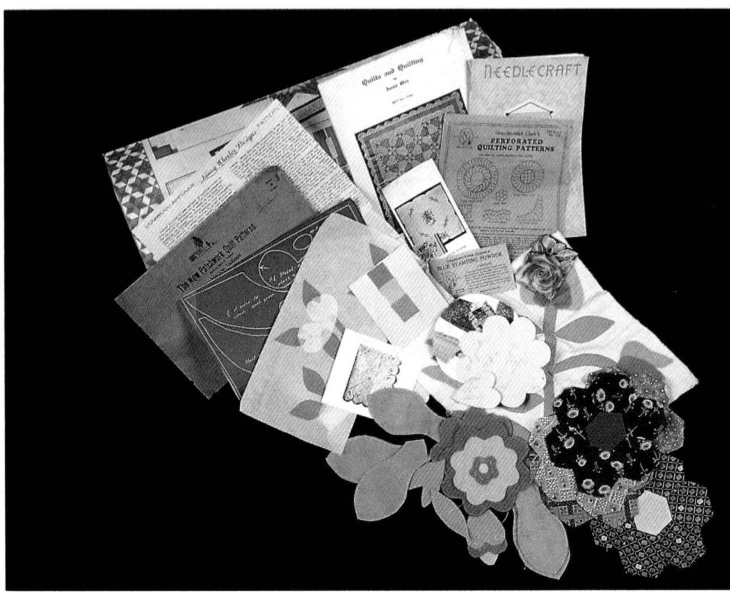

44. Quilt products commonly in use in the quilt revival of the 1930s.

Flora Sexton Wade (? –1968)

Flora Sexton was born in Friendsville, Tennessee, a Quaker community. Trained as a nurse, she took a job at a nearby Knoxville hospital. One night injured and badly burned passengers and workers from a railroad accident arrived at the hospital in ambulances. One of her patients was Joe Wade. They fell in love, married, and lived on Scott Street in Knoxville for the rest of their lives. His hobby was woodworking. Hers was quilting. A group of friends quilted regularly at her house since she could keep a quilt frame up because she had no children.

These columnists, whether they used pseudonyms or their real names, were part of a nationwide advertising trend that created characters like Betty Crocker to offer customers friendly advice about everything from home decorating to halitosis. Nancy Page, Prudence Penny, Laura Wheeler, Aunt Martha, and other quilt columnists replaced the long-time quiltmakers who had passed down traditional patterns and determined standards for quilt construction. For the urban woman, a quiltmaking grandmother was as close as her daily newspaper.

Manufacturers and distributors of sewing notions and gadgets saw the quilt revival as an opportunity to offer new devices to streamline the quiltmaking process. Perforated stencils used with chalk dust or paste saved time in marking intricate quilting designs. Die-cut fabric pieces eliminated the need for cutting pieces by hand. Appliqué quilt kits including fabric and prestamped pieces took the guesswork out of quiltmaking.

Stearns and Foster Company had manufactured rolls of cotton batting since the 1840s but now used new advertising methods in the twentieth-century quilt revival. Their mythical home advisor, Phoebe Edwards, gave advice on how to make a quilt and the company began to show patterns on their batting wrappers. Textile companies offered endless yards of brightly colored or pastel solid and printed cloth at very low prices and advertised directly to quiltmakers through catalogs and magazines.

(continued on page 31)

45. Detail of Colonial Rose, the winner of the second place national prize by Mabel Langley of Dallas, Texas. According to a letter Mabel Langley wrote to Lillie Belle Carpenter, she used pattern no. 1213, Colonial Rose, published by the St. Louis Fancy Work Company of St. Louis, Missouri, and she used a good grade of sateen.

46. Detail of Colonial Rose showing quilting.

47. VASES OF FLOWERS

Maker: Alma Irene Hull Cummings
Scotch Ridge, Iowa, 1933

Appliqué: 86″ x 72″; cotton

Collection of Sharon Kline, granddaughter.

Alma Irene Hull Cummings (1890–1977)

Alma Cummings and her husband, Homer, owned a farm in central Iowa near Des Moines. According to her granddaughter, Alma made several hundred quilts which she gave to family and friends, but she also sold quilts to provide the family with extra income. According to a family story, she entered the Iowa State Fair and won so many prizes for her quilts the officials asked her to stop entering.

48. Alma Irene Hull Cummings, 1939

By 1933, the Sears catalog contained all the latest tools and fabrics any quiltmaker would need: batting, fine imported and domestic cotton, thread, quilting frame clamps, bias binding, quilt kits, ready-cut patches for eight different quilts, and patterns for Double Wedding Ring, Eight-Point Star, Texas Star, Dresden Plate, Round the World, and Basket.[3]

Sears's 1933 sales records are not available for review, but undoubtedly the company experienced increased volume in their quilting items in the early 1930s. The advertising department was undoubtedly well aware of the renewed enthusiasm for the tradition of quiltmaking among both rural and urban customers. Sears saw a national contest as a further way to expand the market for fabric and quilting items. By offering a prize of $1,200, it ignited the American competitive spirit resulting in an explosion of quiltmaking.

AMERICA'S CHAMPION QUILTER

The Contest and the Prize

Sears, Roebuck and Company promoted numerous contests during the 1920s and 1930s. Company leaders believed that a positive corporate image, coupled with creative philanthropy, generated both good will and good sales. Improvement in customers' lives meant improved economics for Sears. Contests spotlighted problems and rewarded contestants who came up with solutions. Typical was the 1925 Sears National Seed-Corn Show, in which the best ear of corn from 27,411 entries brought its owner a cash prize of one thousand dollars, with smaller awards for runners-up. Sears's ultimate goal was to encourage farmers to test their seed before planting to improve crop yield.

Other contests included the National Single-Stalk Cotton Show in 1928 with prizes totaling ten thousand dollars and the National Canning Contest in 1929, which attracted 43,000 entries from farm women. In 1930 the 4-H Club Scenario-Writing Contest attracted 2,000 entries and the Home Beautiful Contest, 47,000. With each contest, Sears encouraged better farming techniques, improved home management, and development of farm youth. In return, the company maintained a highly positive profile in farming communities. Using a quilt contest as a public relations vehicle linked Sears with a beloved traditional American craft that was experiencing a revival in the early 1930s.

The Century of Progress managers viewed contests as a means to increase fair attendance in the midst of the Great

49. Practice blocks and stuffed stripping for grand prize winning quilt entered by Margaret Rogers Caden.

1833 A CENTURY OF PROGRESS 1933

MAKE Sears BUILDING YOUR HEADQUARTERS WHEN YOU VISIT THE WORLD'S FAIR

IMPORTANT POINTS *of* INTEREST *at the* FAIR

1. ADLER PLANETARIUM
2. AGRICULTURAL GROUP
3. SKY RIDE
4. ELECTRICAL GROUP
5. SHEDD AQUARIUM
6. ADMINISTRATION BUILDING
7. SEARS-ROEBUCK BUILDING
8. HALL OF SCIENCE
9. FIELD MUSEUM
10. SOLDIER FIELD

The vast Sears family of customers and friends will have headquarters of its own at Chicago's 1933 World's Fair, "A Century of Progress." A big, attractive, comfortable building where they can meet, rest, eat, write—in short, where they can feel perfectly "at home." You will be more than welcome.

The Fair will be open June 1 to November 1 and will outstrip in size and in interesting exhibits, its illustrious predecessor of '93, the World's Columbian Exposition.

In the very midst of the world's wonders, just inside one of the main gateways, we have built the beautiful structure pictured above, for your comfort and convenience.

Here you will find lounging quarters, rest rooms, check-room facilities, a complete information bureau to tell you about roads, railroads, and local transportation, and a telephone and telegraph office.

CENTURY OF PROGRESS

QUILTING CONTEST

$7,500 IN PRIZES

Do you quilt? If you do, you'll be interested in entering Sears great nationwide Quilting Contest, being held in connection with the Chicago World's Fair. Anyone may enter a quilt in this contest. At the close of the contest the winning quilts will be exhibited in the Sears building at the Fair.

For full particulars, write Sue Roberts, Home Advisor, for free circular 9452L. Address your letter to your nearest Sears mail order house.

The broad expanse of roof has been made into a delightful open deck overlooking a large portion of the grounds and swept by the refreshing breezes of Lake Michigan. There will be interesting exhibits of merchandise and manufacturing processes. They will be highly informative, you will enjoy them thoroughly, and you'll not be asked to buy!

The Sears building and the many free services it provides are yours while you're at the Fair. Use them; make this your headquarters; we want you to come and feel at ease.

If there is any special information you would like to have in advance of coming to the Fair, we will be glad to get it for you; and we will send you free on request a circular published by the Fair management, describing and picturing various buildings and other attractions. Please address your request to our nearest Mail Order House.

50. Inside front cover of Sears catalog, January 1933, inviting Sears customers to visit the Sears Building at the Century of Progress Fair. Note also the announcement of the quilting contest.

Depression. Thus they acquiesced when, in the fall of 1932, Sears executives asked for official sanction for a quilt contest. J. H. White, Sears's divisional sales manager of Domestics and Bedspreads, requested permission to advertise the promotion through its nearly four hundred retail stores, seven million spring catalogs, and twelve million January sale catalogs. He added, "We believe this contest will provide a tremendous amount of publicity for the Fair and ourselves . . . [and] greatly add to the value and the prestige to both of us."[1]

Since "the exposition has from time to time received inquiries as to whether any showing of quilts was to be made and in view of the fact that these inquiries are constantly coming in," Ed Ross Bartley, director of the fair's Department of Promotion, granted Sears the official sponsorship of the Century of Progress Quilt Contest.[2]

Sears's January sale catalogs carried a page-one announcement for the company's exhibit building at the fair. A box at the bottom of the page inquired, "Do you quilt?" and offered the incentive of $7,500 in prize money. Quilters were invited to send for a flier, which listed rules and prizes under the tantalizing headline, "Think What Winning the Grand Prize Would Mean!" Rules were few. Each contestant could enter only one quilt. Quilts had to be bed-sized and the work of the entrants. "Anyone may enter by submitting a complete patchwork quilt of his or her own making which has never been previously exhibited." Entries could be either "of original or traditional

51. Contest information brochure and entry form. Collection of Charles Fitzgerald and Margaret McDonald.

design." A note in small print encouraged people to enter recently made quilts: "It is NOT our intention to make this an exhibit of antiques and heirlooms."

Prizes were offered in a series of heats, beginning at the local store level with five- and ten-dollar prizes and progressing through ten regional semifinals with prizes of twenty-five, seventy-five, and two hundred dollars. The top thirty quilts (three from each regional semifinal) would be selected for exhibit at the fair where they would be judged and the "grand national prize" of $1,000 awarded. Further encouragement for modern quiltmaking was the offer of a bonus of $200 if the top quilt was an "original design commemorating the Century of Progress Exposition."[3]

The deadline for entries was midnight, May 15, 1933, allowing about four months to design and complete a new quilt. Many women entered recently completed needlework, but many others set to work on new quilts.

The $1,200 combination of first prize and bonus was a strong incentive. In 1933 a luxury car such as a Dodge V-8 cost $1,115; a new Ford, $490; a three-bedroom house, $3,000. Translated into today's dollars, the award equals about $20,000.

52. CORNUCOPIA

Maker: Marie Mueller
Garnavillo, Iowa, 1933

Appliqué: Cotton

Collection of Ardis and Robert James

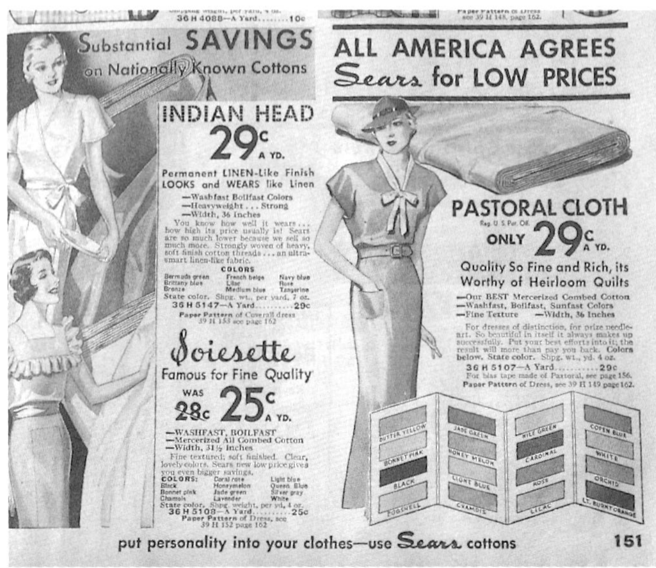

53. From Sears catalog, 1935, advertising pastoral cloth in solid colors.

Marie Mueller of Garnavillo, Iowa, made a new quilt for the contest, choosing a Cornucopia design. Although the contest rules did not dictate that entrants use Sears fabric, Marie purchased several yards of pastoral cloth, which she saw advertised in the 1933 catalog at the extravagant price of twenty-five cents per yard, when color-fast percale was only twelve cents. The catalog maintained that the colors for pastoral cloth "were chosen with blending in mind. Blue harmonizes with the deeper blue, Nile green with dark green, etc. . . . Many a prize-winning quilt will be made from this fine cotton."[4]

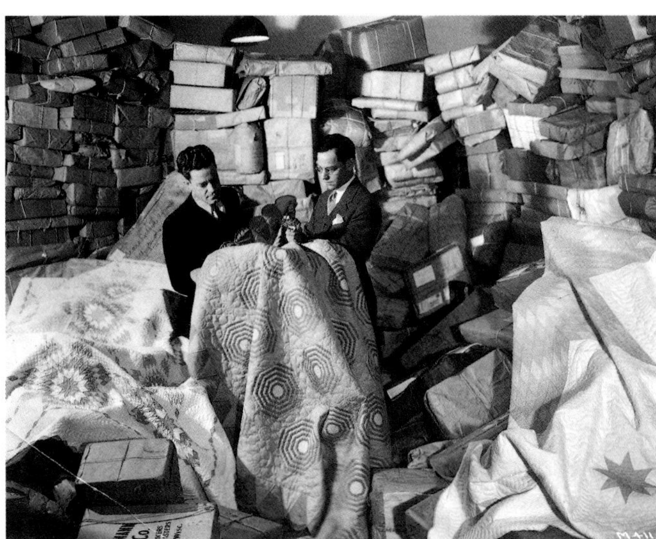

54. Sears officials in Chicago were deluged with packages containing contest quilts. E. J. Condon, director of public relations *(left)* and George Vidal examine stitches with a magnifying glass. Photograph courtesy of Sears Archives.

The expense for the pastoral cloth was a good investment, Marie thought, and it certainly could not hurt her chances to win. She finished the Cornucopia in time to deliver it to her local store by May 15. Although she did not win a prize, she received a green ribbon, an award of merit, which is still with the quilt. It may be that these green ribbons were special awards. Marie Mueller wrote, "I was real happy at the time to be recognized, as by the grapevine I had heard of a lady sending in a quilt and only getting the quilt back."[5]

It is also possible that every entrant received a green ribbon as a contest souvenir. Such universal awards may have been a tradition with Sears since all entries in its World's Fair Canning Contest, for example, won a lithographed certificate suitable for framing.

Had Marie Mueller's quilt won one of the three top prizes at her local store, it would have progressed to a semifinal at a big-city Sears store in Chicago, Philadelphia, Boston, Kansas City, Minneapolis, Memphis, Atlanta, Dallas, Los Angeles, or Seattle. Marie was but one of 24,878 people who responded to Sears's call for quilts, with the promise of a cash prize equivalent to a sum greater than the annual income of the average family.

The publicity department at Sears made the most of the response, flashing a press release around the country with a deluge of statistics. It announced that 25,000 women had spent 5,625,000 hours to make the quilts entered in the contest. The figures were based on the estimate that a quilt required 225 hours or about twenty-eight eight-hour days to complete. "Translated further, that time is equal to 234,875 days or 642 years." The press release described a

55. Lois Hobgood, 1930

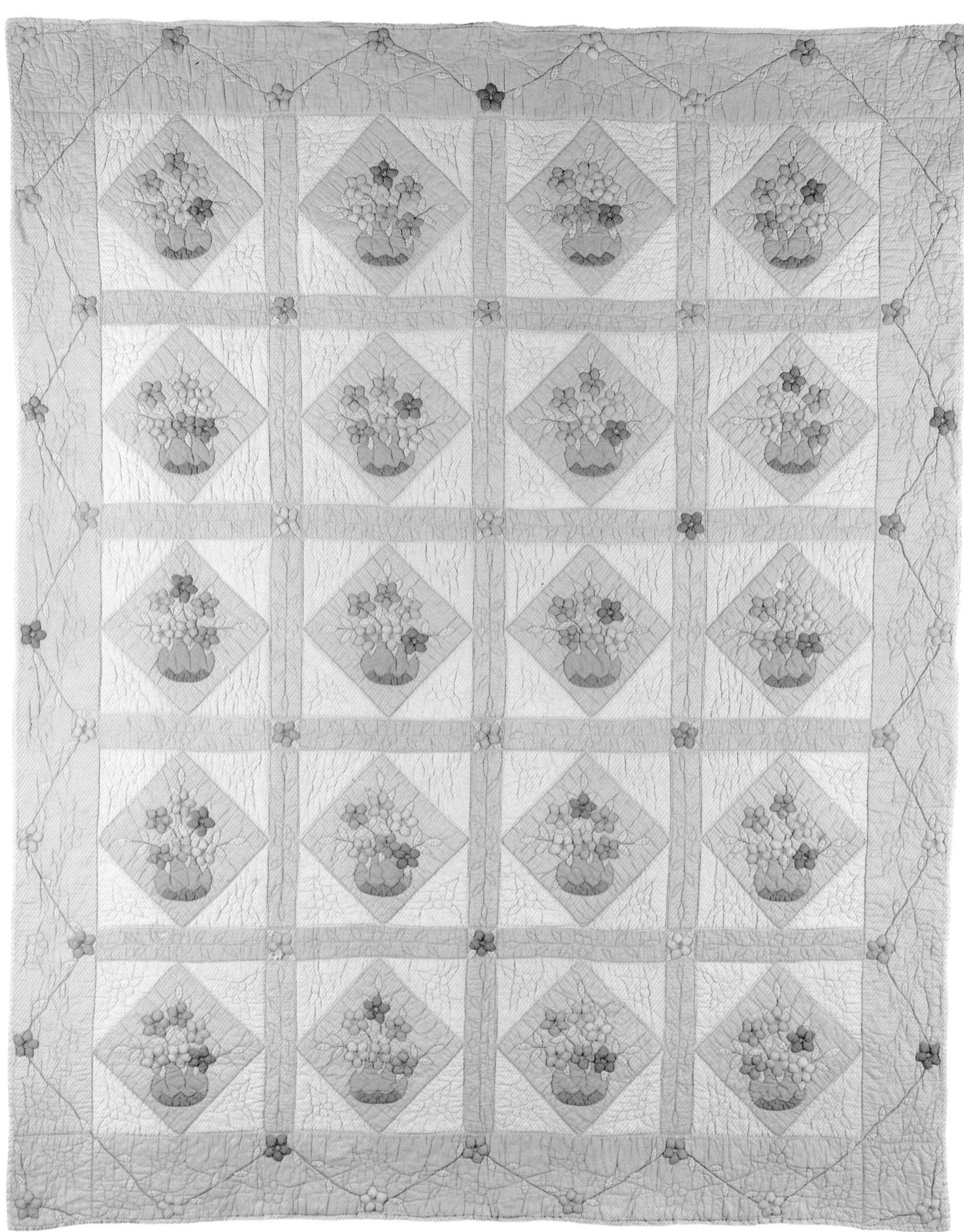

56. BOWL OF FLOWERS

Maker: Lois Hobgood Crowell (b. 1909) with assistance from Fay Underwood
Paluxy, Texas, 1933

Appliquéd, Embroidered, and Pieced: 85″ x 65″; cotton

This quilt won third prize at the Dallas regional contest and was shown at the 1933 Chicago World's Fair.

Collection of Lois Hobgood Crowell.

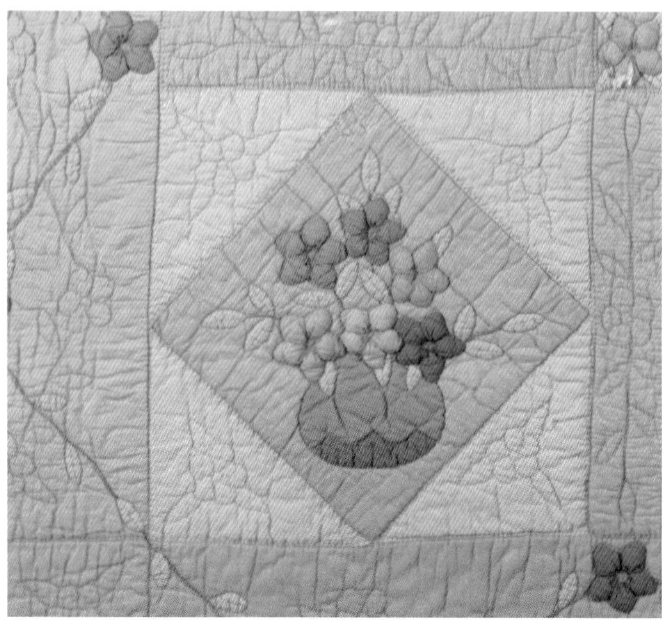

57. Detail of Bowl of Flowers

twelve-foot-tall mountain of packages at the Chicago mail-order house where quilts shipped in cartons, hat boxes, and old suitcases formed a pile one hundred feet in circumference at the base.

Sixty years later, the Sears contest remains the largest quilt competition ever held. Compare it to another national contest, sponsored by *Good Housekeeping* in 1978, during another revival of interest in quiltmaking. First prize then was $2,500, a relatively smaller sum but the largest cash prize yet awarded. Jinny Beyer was the winner with her Ray of Light, a heavily quilted central medallion. The 1978 contest attracted 9,954 entries, fewer than half as many as in 1933. In 1986 the Museum of American Folk Art held another national quilt contest to commemorate the centennial of the Statue of Liberty. The $20,000 won by Moneca Calvert with her Glorious Lady Freedom, a dramatic pictorial design, is still the record for a cash prize, roughly equivalent in value to the Sears award fifty years earlier. However, the 1986 contest inspired only a few thousand entries.

Sears's prize money was just part of the incentive for Texas entrant Lois Hobgood Crowell. When she saw the quilt contest announcement in her January 1933 catalog, she had never quilted a quilt. With the self-assurance only a twenty-three-year-old could possess, she decided she was capable of making a prize winner the first time she tried.

Lois Hobgood was teaching school in the town of Paluxy, where there was little money or entertainment. Making a quilt sounded like inexpensive fun. She confided her ambition to a friend, Fay Underwood, who was immediately skeptical that Lois could make a quilt, let alone win a prize. Lois retorted, "I've got two hands, don't I?"

"I knew that to win, the quilt pattern would really have to be outstanding," she recalled in 1983, "so I searched for the perfect pattern." She liked the idea of a floral motif, but nothing caught her eye. With characteristic confidence, she designed her own pattern, sketching a bowl of flowers set on the diagonal. She asked the advice of a Sears home economist, a service offered by several stores in the months leading up to the deadline. After looking at the pattern and the proposed color scheme, the professional offered suggestions. Lois recalled:

> And it's a good thing she did. The colors in my original design had too much contrast. She showed me how to tone it down and blend the colors together. And, you know, when I got my judges' rating form back on that quilt, I saw I lost everything on the quilting, it being my first quilt. But I got 100 percent on design and color, and that's what won it for me.

Lois Hobgood made excellent use of the pastel palette typical of the 1930s. Choosing a color scheme of peach and pale green, she stuffed each of the pastel flowers for a three-dimensional effect.

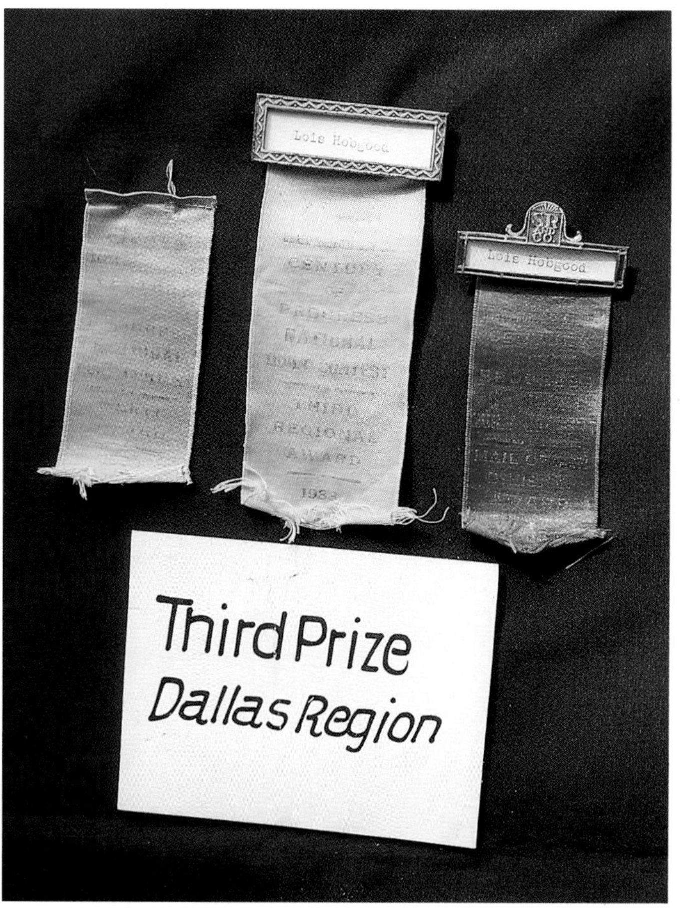

58. Ribbons won by Lois Hobgood at the Dallas regional contest: a green merit award, a yellow third regional award, and a blue mail-order division award. The description card hung on her quilt while in Chicago.

Her doubting friend Fay helped to sew in the evenings after school, and her boyfriend (later her husband) helped stuff the flower petals during his visits. Lois remembered the quiltmaking as more of a social event than a job, as they worked on it only if there was nothing else they would rather do.

When the top was ready for the frame, the two women were ready to learn to quilt. Lois lived next door to a professional quilter and had watched her work, picking up some techniques. She could have hired her neighbor to quilt the top, "and she would have done a fabulous job for five or six dollars, but of course that wouldn't have satisfied me."

As a woman who lived far from a retail store, Lois Hobgood sent her entry to one of ten mail-order centers. The closest was Dallas, where she won a local prize of ten dollars. The quilt then moved to the regional contest at the Dallas store, where—to everyone's surprise but hers—it took third place and a twenty-five dollar award. When the two checks arrived, Lois gave the smaller one to Fay and spent the larger amount in one lump sum. "I bought a cedar chest to keep that quilt in."

Like the twenty-nine other regional winners, Lois's quilt went on to the Sears Pavilion at the Century of Progress Exposition. Her brother, who was living with her in Paluxy, visited the fair. Although he insisted he was sick of quilts, the topic that dominated all conversation in the household that spring, he toured the Sears building and saw his sister's quilt in its place of glory.[6]

Lillie Belle Carpenter of Hyndman, Pennsylvania, approached the challenge of winning a prize from a different perspective. Rather than designing her own quilt, she ordered a kit from a Chicago mail-order company in April, only one month before the entry deadline. The Rising Sun quilt was a new design by H. Ver Mehren of Des Moines who sold patterns through his own Home Art Company and the Needleart Company in Chicago. Their catalogs offered all of the material needed for the top and border ready-stamped on four shades of sateen, gingham, or inexpensive cleona cloth from $5.95 down to $3.50. Color choices were four harmonizing shades of pink, blue, orchid, and yellow.[7] Lillie Belle Carpenter chose yellow, the shade illustrated in the catalog.

The contest rules said nothing about entering quilts made from commercial patterns or kits, which were an important part of the quilt market from the 1920s through the 1960s. Kits offered fabric with the cutting lines stamped on the material; and some took the process one step further, giving the seamstress die-cut pieces.

Mrs. Carpenter did not design her pattern, blend her fabrics, or mark the cutting lines. Her genius was the choice of a show-stopping design and the feat of finishing a complex pattern from kit to bound quilt in about a month. The family does not recall if she quilted the top alone (she used H. Ver Mehren's quilting designs), but she must have had help with the intricate quilting to have met the deadline at the Philadelphia Sears mail-order house.

Having won one of five top prizes in the mail-order division, on May 25 Mrs. Carpenter's quilt competed for a ten-dollar prize in the semifinals at Sears's Roosevelt Boulevard store in Philadelphia. On May 27 she received a letter from Sue Roberts, home advisor at Sears's Chicago headquarters, telling her she had won the regional first prize of $200.

Lillie Belle Shaffer Carpenter (1877–1945)

At the time of the contest, Lillie Belle and her husband were living on a farm growing potatoes, vegetables, and "a little bit of everything," according to her son Herbert. She liked outdoor work better than her household chores, but she made very special quilts. Her goal was to have every stitch exactly the same as the next. Her brother Lloyd encouraged her to enter the contest and even bought her the fabric and batting. After she won, she gave the quilt to him. Her son went to the fair to see the quilt exhibit. He said it was a very proud moment. Lillie Belle kept dozens of letters and newspaper clippings about the contest that served as a valuable resource for this book.

59. Lillie Belle Shaffer Carpenter

60. SUNBURST

Maker: Lillie Belle Shaffer Carpenter
Hyndman, Pennsylvania, 1933

Pieced: Cotton

This is an exact duplicate of the quilt that won first prize in the Philadelphia regional contest and was shown at the Chicago World's Fair.

Collection of Carl Carpenter, son.

Chicago headquarters allowed some freedom to each regional executive to run the local contest as he wished. Many announced the finalists with a good deal of hoopla, placing news stories in home-town newspapers and buying display advertisements that invited customers to visit the store to see the prize-winning quilts.

L. W. Thompson was contest manager for the eastern region, headquartered at the Philadelphia store. In his press release he emphasized the significance of Lillie Belle Carpenter's prize: her quilt was the best of 1,700 quilts entered from women in eight states (records indicate Philadelphia received quilts from New York, New Jersey, Pennsylvania, Ohio, Maryland, West Virginia, and North Carolina). He invited Philadelphians to view the top three quilts for a few days in early June before the prize winners were shipped to Chicago.

This focusing of attention on the quiltmaker made Lillie Belle Carpenter's prize the biggest event of her lifetime. "We believe this contest of ours was a good thing and we want everyone to know about the presentation of the prize," Thompson wrote her, telling of his plans to present to her a check for $210 in a ceremony at the Grange Hall in her hometown before an audience of her friends and neighbors. L. W. Thompson and his wife drove to Hyndman in mid-June and spent the afternoon of the official presentation with the Carpenters, who, after meeting him, told him he was now considered family.[8]

Her Skillful Hands

I see her sitting by a quilting frame;
I see her shining needle weaving a pattern;
She does not think her work will make for her a name
Or that a lot of money she might earn.

'Twas just a bit of handwork for a brother;
'Twas just another act of helpfulness and love;
'Twas just a bit from the dull life of a mother;
'Twas just another accomplishment to approve.

I see her hands as they skillfully stitch, stitch, stitch.
Oh no, you would say, they are not very pretty,
Not soft, tapering, and white like the idle rich
But hands of a farmer's wife who does her duty.

It is the old, old story proven once again,
Using one's intellect and one's hand for service;
A fully rich, most abundant life you attain
And thru the hardship comes the rising sun of bliss.

Written in honor of Mrs. Virgil W. Carpenter's prize-winning quilt by Mildred S. Carpenter on June 15, 1933.

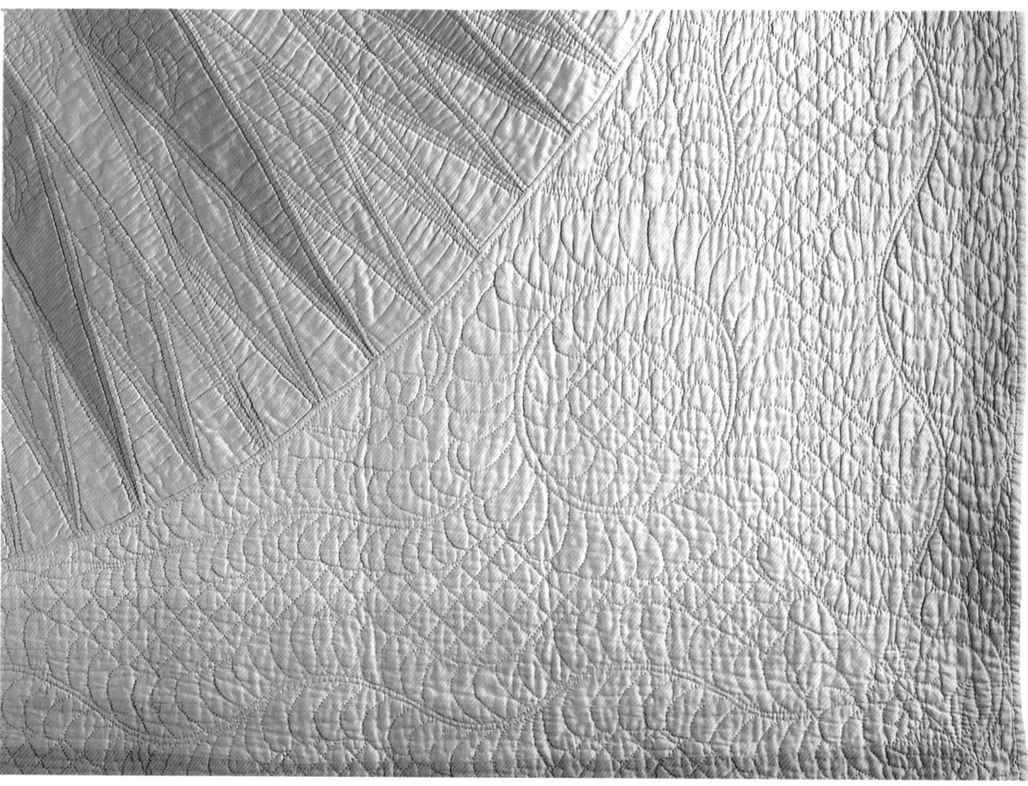

61. Detail of Sunburst

62. *Colonial Quilts* booklet of patterns designed by H. Ver Mehren of Des Moines, Iowa, and sold through the Home Art Company and the Needleart Company of Chicago.

For the event, a family member wrote a poem in honor of the hands that made the Rising Sun quilt, which the family called Sunburst.

Mrs. Carpenter received congratulatory letters from fellow quilters who had entered but did not win, along with requests for her pattern. She in turn corresponded with other prize winners asking for their patterns. At one time she planned to make a copy of the top three quilts at the fair. The correspondence from Sears and other quiltmakers has been preserved by Lillie Belle Carpenter's family, who still treasure the contest memorabilia and her prize-winning quilt.

In early June 1933 Mrs. Carpenter's Sunburst, Lois Hobgood's Bowl of Flowers, and twenty-eight other quilts competed in the finals for the $1,000 first prize. Sears had earlier announced the national judges as Mary McElwain, owner of the Mary McElwain Quilt Shop in Walworth, Wisconsin; Anne Orr, the needlework editor of *Good Housekeeping;* Sue Roberts, Sears home advisor and contest organizer; Robert B. Harshe, director of the Art Institute of Chicago; and Mrs. Charles Sewell, an employee of the American Farm Bureau Federation. At the actual judging, Mrs. Sewell was not present and Robert Harshe was replaced by his assistant, Beth Burnett.

The judges awarded the first prize to a quilt described in the initial publicity as an Unknown Star, entered by Margaret Rogers Caden of Lexington, Kentucky. They gave the second prize of $500 to Mabel Langley of Dallas, Texas, for her Colonial Rose and the third prize of $300 to Frida V. Plume of Evanston, Illinois, for a red and white quilt in the pattern known as Delectable Mountains. Two quilts received honorable mention, an Autumn Leaf by Mary A. Hilliker of Carl Junction, Missouri, and a Star of France by Susie Combs of Pebworth, Kentucky.

The top three winners were traditional patterns, remarkably made. The judges obviously valued expert stitching above color, design, and creativity, the last characteristic seeming to have ranked lowest on their scale. Three of the five quilts they honored were made from commercial patterns or kits.

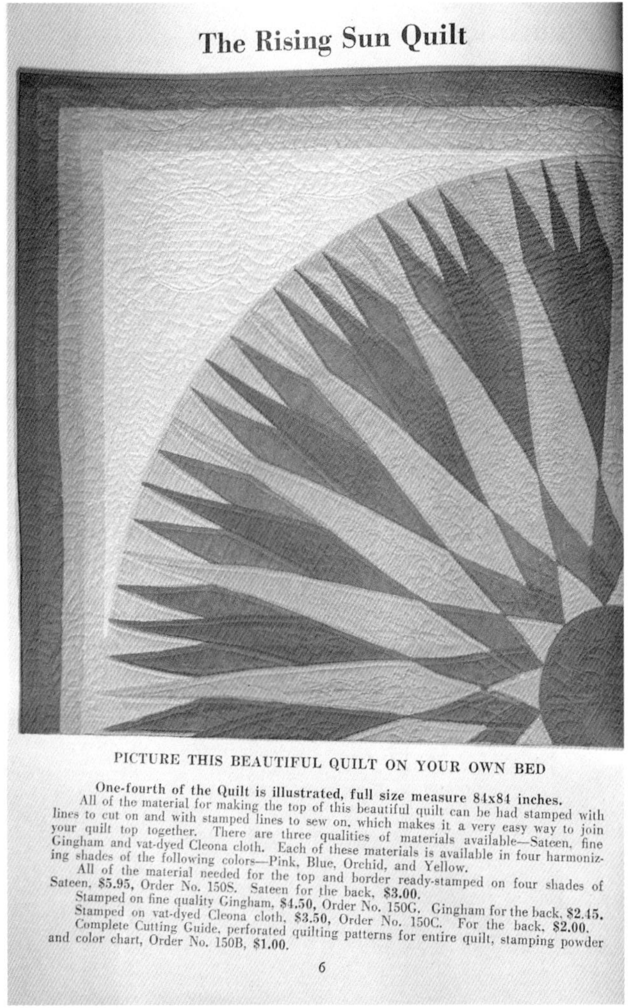

63. Advertising for Rising Sun pattern in *Colonial Quilts*.

64. Judges for the Philadelphia regional contest *(left to right):* Mrs. William E. Linglebach, president of the Philadelphia Federation of Women's Clubs; Bernard Davis, president of the LaFrance Textile Industries of Philadelphia; and Mrs. Caroline King, women's editor of *Country Gentleman*. Photograph courtesy of H. M. Carpenter.

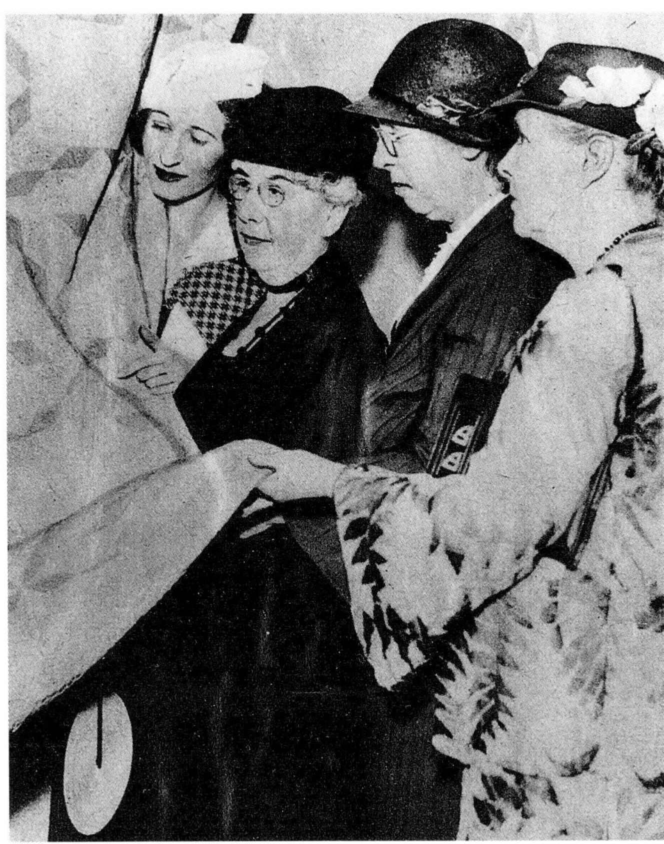

65. Final round judges: Sue Roberts of Sears, Roebuck, and Company; quilt designer Anne Orr; shop owner Mary McElwain; and Beth Burnett, assistant to the director of the Chicago Art Institute. They are examining the grand prize-winning quilt at the 1933 Century of Progress Exposition. Photograph courtesy of Spencer Museum of Art.

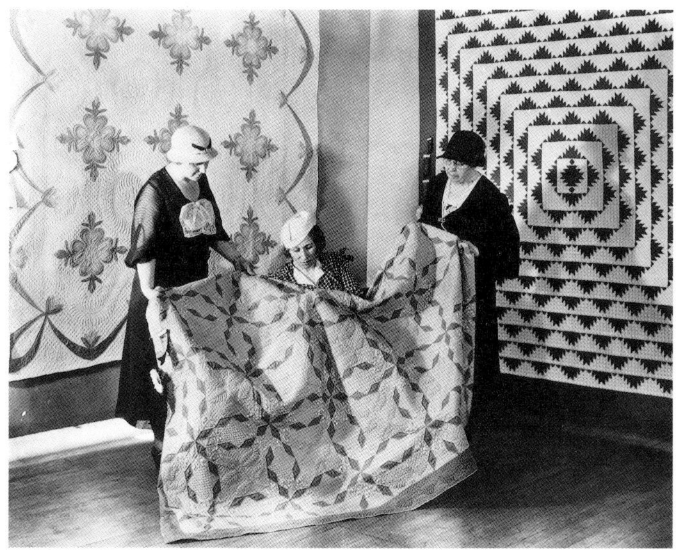

66. Sears contest judges examine grand prize-winning quilt. On the wall are the second prize winner, Colonial Rose, by Mabel Langley, Dallas, Texas, and the third prize winner, Delectable Mountains, by Frida Plume of Evanston, Illinois. Photograph courtesy of Sears Archives.

Ida M. Stow, a disgruntled contestant, took Sears to task for the judges' taste in a June 1933 letter. She felt they were biased against the quilts that commemorated the fair in unique designs. One judge had been overheard to state that "she would not give three minutes of her time to the Century of Progress designs."[9]

Sears had formulated the contest rules and then chose four judges with opinions that differed from those of the contest's original organizers. The judges favored traditional patterns, and the $200 bonus for the Century of Progress commemorative was never awarded.

Judge and contest coordinator Sue Roberts described her personal preferences in a letter to William R. Dunton, a quilt historian. "They [the commemoratives] are very decorative, and as commemorative quilts, unusual and striking, but I still prefer the more orthodox variety, don't you."[10]

67. Autumn Leaves by Mary Hilliker of Carl Junction, Missouri, won one of only two honorable mention awards in the final round of judging. Photograph courtesy of Sears Archives.

68. LOUISIANA ROSE

Maker: Celia Pardue Hyde
Crowley, Louisiana, 1930–33

Appliqué: 84″ x 81″; cotton sateen

The quilt won second prize in the Dallas regional contest and was shown at the 1933 Chicago World's Fair.

Collection of Marjorie Malone, niece.

69. Celia Pardue Hyde, circa 1930

Celia Pardue Hyde (1881–1972)

Celia Pardue graduated from Louisiana State Normal College in 1903 and taught in the public schools of Louisiana for several years. In 1918 she married Dr. Wendel Hyde and moved to Crowley, Louisiana. Her hobbies from early childhood included all types of needlework: embroidery, tatting, crocheting, and quiltmaking. In later life she took up oil and watercolor painting.

The Quilt of the Century

Margaret Caden's grand prize-winning quilt was a perfect example of "the orthodox variety." The design itself, a traditional Diamond Star, was rather undistinguished despite its impeccable piecing. The fabrics were shades of the pale gray-green so popular during the 1930s. Its distinctive aspect was intricate stuffed quilting, which must have strongly influenced the judges despite the fact that quilting counted only forty out of a possible one hundred points on the official scorecard. Fifty years later, Marie Mueller remembered it well. "The first prize quilt . . . was quilted sixteen stitches to the inch which was outstanding."[11] Her praise echoed that of judge Sue Roberts: "A detail picture is really better than one of the entire quilt for it shows the stuffed quilting, which is really the outstanding feature of it."[12]

Louise Fowler Roote, quilt columnist for *Capper's Weekly,* described the Caden quilt to her readers:

> It was the handsomest piece of needlework imaginable. Swathed in cellophane, it hung suspended full length in the display room of Sears and Roebuck's exposition along with dozens of other gorgeous specimens, and on it proudly fluttered the prize ribbon. . . . It was really the remarkable padded quilting which made this quilt so exquisite.[13]

Today our perspective on the beauty of the prize-winning quilt must be obtained through the words of those who saw it during the fair's first season, as first lady Eleanor Roosevelt accepted The Unknown Star as a gift after the fair closed in 1933, and no records of the quilt

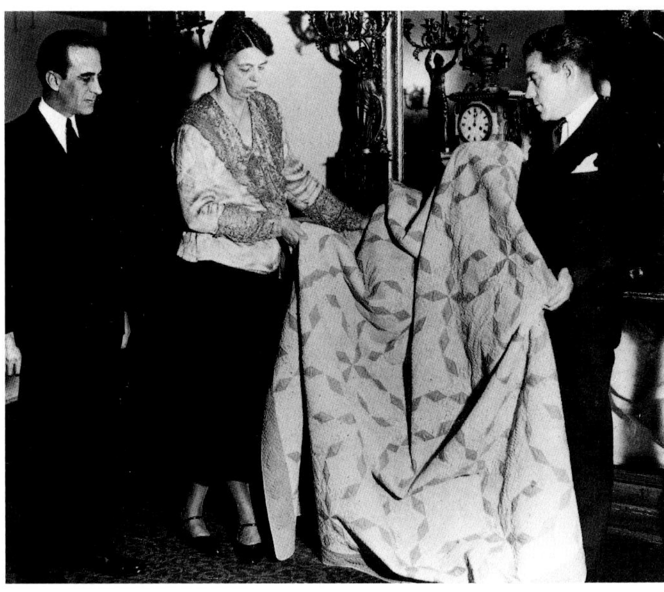

70. E. J. Condon of Sears presents the grand prize-winning quilt to Mrs. Eleanor Roosevelt. The whereabouts of the quilt today is unknown. Photograph courtesy of Sears Archives.

71. FLORIDIAN GARDEN

Maker: Louella Beatty Bitter
Quincy, Illinois, 1933

Appliqué and Embroidery: 90″ x 68″; silk

Collection of Eleanor Alford, granddaughter.

72. Detail of Floridian Garden, showing embroidery.

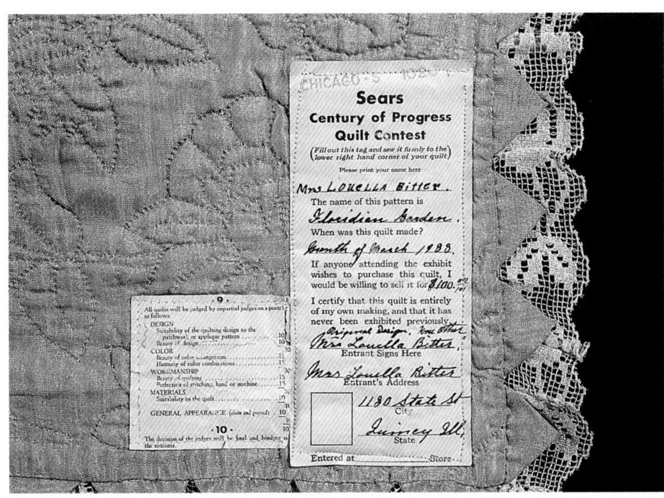

74. Standards used for judging the Sears contest quilts.

73. Dr. J. W. E. Bitter and Louella Beatty Bitter, Quincy, Illinois, in 1936.

Louella Beatty Bitter (1861–1954)

Louella Bitter and her husband, Dr. J. W. Edward Bitter, a prominent Quincy, Illinois, physician, had a winter home in St. Petersburg, Florida. This quilt, made in March 1933, celebrates Louella's love for Florida's tropical plants and birds. An accomplished artist in oils, charcoal, and pastels, Louella designed the appliqué and quilting designs. According to family tradition, the quilt was disqualified because the French knots had worked through the silk.

THIS QUILT WON THE THOUSAND DOLLAR PRIZE

75. From *Capper's Weekly,* May 26, 1934

76. Margaret Rogers Caden, Lexington, Kentucky, grand prize winner in the 1933 Sears Quilt Contest.

exist after 1934. Because laws governing presidential gifts had not yet been passed, Mrs. Roosevelt was free to keep it or give it away, a gesture she frequently made with other White House gifts, including at least one other quilt sent to her while her husband was president.

Many replicas of the "Quilt of the Century" survive. After the fair, several commercial sources sold patterns and kits with advertisements that lauded Margaret Rogers Caden. Her hometown newspaper hailed her as "America's Champion Quilter," praise that must have benefited the needlework business she ran with her sisters.[14]

The week the fair opened in Chicago, the A. M. Caden Gift Shop ran a display ad in the *Lexington Herald,* promoting its selection of wedding and commencement gifts. Merchandise included linen handkerchiefs, smocked dresses, pillow shams, custom draperies, and handmade quilts. Even before the fair, the Cadens' shop had a national reputation as an elite establishment catering to Lexington's horse-racing set. At one point the shop maintained a branch in Miami Beach during the winter months and one in Saratoga Springs, New York, during the racing season. A surviving pair of elegant silk quilts from the Caden shop was commissioned by the Fisher family, whose fortune came from the Fisher bodies of General Motors cars, evidence of the Cadens' quality merchandise and choice clientele.

Ann M. Caden ran the shop in downtown Lexington. She and her five sisters, Elizabeth, Mame, Margaret, Sue, and Alice, all single women, lived together in the family home. Elizabeth kept house; Sue was a nurse; and Alice worked in a drugstore. Mame and Margaret worked with Ann.

(continued on page 54)

Quilt of the Century

Twinkle, twinkle, quilted star,
Now I wonder how you are
Pieced and padded, oh so high,
For the White House by and by!
"This Quilt Won the Thousand Dollar Prize,"

—*Capper's Weekly,* May 26, 1934

77. STAR OF THE BLUEGRASS

Maker: Unknown
Probably made in the 1940s

Pieced: 90″ x 77″; cotton

This quilt, made from a 1940s Stearns and Foster pattern, duplicates the grand prize-winning quilt entered by Margaret Rogers Caden of Lexington, Kentucky. Missing in this quilt is the padded quilting for which the Caden quilt received so much praise.

Collection of Stearns Technical Textiles Company.

78. Detail of Star of the Bluegrass (made in the 1940s)

79. NEW YORK BEAUTY

Maker: Pieced by Rose Tekippe and quilted by the Twelve Faithful Quilters
Fort Atkinson, Iowa, 1932

Pieced: 79″ x 79″; cotton

The quilt won third prize in the Minneapolis regional contest and was shown at the 1933 Chicago World's Fair.

Collection of Ada Tekippe Schlick, sister.

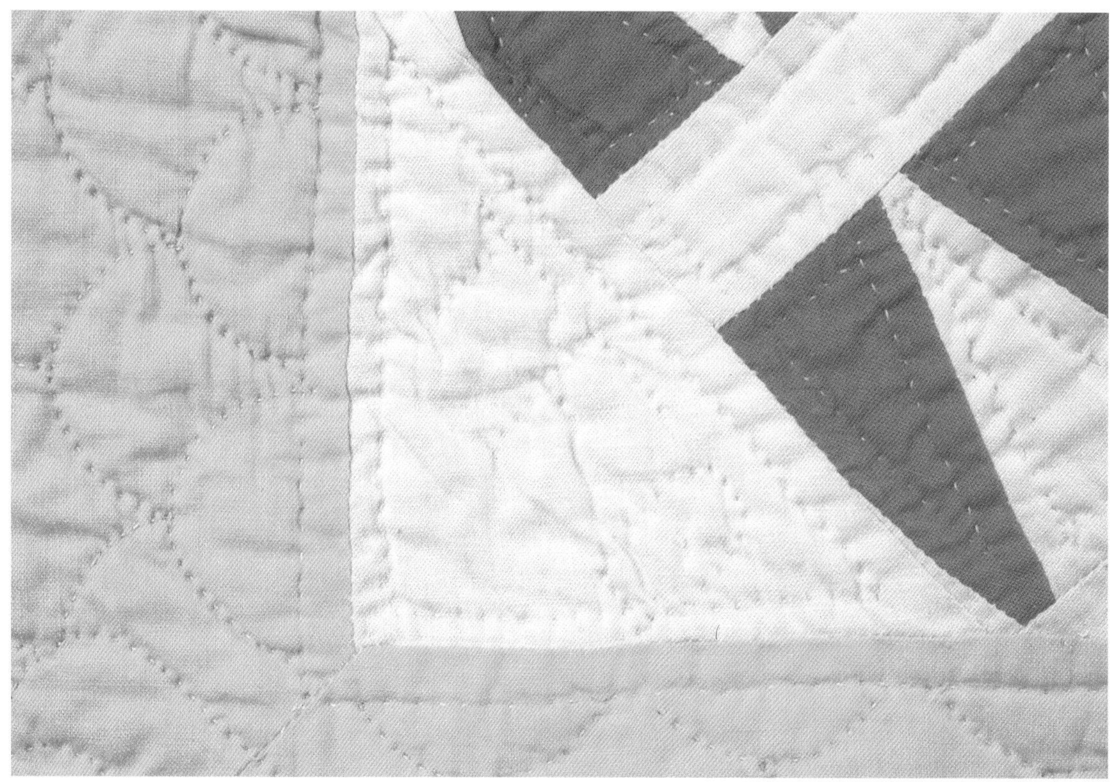

80. In one corner are the initials "TFQ," signifying the Twelve Faithful Quilters. The other corners are marked "May 2," the year "1932," and "R. Tekippe."

81. Rose Tekippe

Rose Tekippe (1901–1992)

Rose Tekippe graduated from nurses' training in 1926 and passed her Iowa State Board exams soon after. She worked for a time at St. Joseph's Hospital in New Hampton, Iowa, but also took on private cases. Rose began quilting after her mother was caught up in the 1930s quilt revival. They prided themselves on the tiny quilting stitches in this quilt. Three quilts were sent to the Sears contest from Rose, her mother, and her sister, but only Rose's quilt won a prize. This prize-winning quilt was pieced by Rose but was quilted at her home by a local quilting club named TFQ, meaning "Twelve Faithful Quilters."

(continued from page 49)

Besides offering finished quilts as part of the needlework selection, the Caden sisters took orders to quilt customers' tops, a task subcontracted to rural quilters. The gift shop also sold quilt patterns. Within a month of receiving her award, Margaret Caden was selling patterns and fabric for her contest quilt, which she now called the Star of the Bluegrass. She offered mail-order customers a choice of "Scotch gingham like the prize quilt for $15.00" or "Ever-fast gingham for $8.50."[15]

The Star of the Bluegrass was undoubtedly an exquisite example of a Caden quilt; but like others from the shop, it was not the work of Margaret Caden, whose quiltmaking was limited to orchestrating the work of the seamstresses who sewed for hire. The Cadens' usual procedure was to commission one woman to sew the patchwork top and then send it to a woman in Owsley County southeast of Lexington, who hired a professional quilter to finish it. For this quilt, the Cadens hired a third seamstress who stuffed the leaves in the plain blocks and borders, the padded quilting described by those who saw it as "exquisite" and "outstanding."

Several Kentucky women recall the story of the making of the Star of the Bluegrass.[16] Mattie Clark Black of Lexington told her daughter-in-law, Helen Black, how she stuffed featherlike leaf designs into green strips and squares on a commission from Margaret Caden. Louise Rhorer Eddleman of Springfield remembered her mother, Ida Atchison Rhorer, piecing the top, using a pattern and fabric given to her by Margaret Caden. Ida Rhorer also received borders, squares, and sashing embellished with padded feathers, which she pieced among the stars. These were undoubtedly the pieces that Mattie Black had stuffed.

Elberta Mainous Botner of Frankfort remembers her mother, Ellen Mainous, acting as a "quilting agent" for the Cadens. She gave the star quilt top with the stuffed leaves to Allie Taylor Price. Ruth Price Stewart of Booneville, Kentucky, remembers the last link in the chain. She, her mother, and her sisters added the crosshatch quilting behind the stuffed work.

83. Ellen Mainous with her husband, Robert

82. Mollie Petit, Willie Clark, Foster Clark, and their sister, Mattie Clark Black *(left to right)*.

Ellen Mainous mailed the finished quilt to the A. M. Caden Gift Shop and Margaret Caden signed the statement on the Sears contest entry form: "I certify that this quilt is entirely of my own making." She stitched the form to the back of the quilt and shipped the piece to the Sears mail-order house in Chicago.

Mattie Black (1885–1963), who stuffed the leaves, supported her family during the Depression with her fine sewing because her husband, James, was unable to support the family. In addition to their everyday living expenses, she paid college tuition for a son and daughter with the money she earned from smocking children's clothes, tailoring draperies, and piecing quilt tops.

The story of Ida Rhorer (1884–1974) is similar. Her husband, Tom, was disabled and she supported the family with her needlework, earning twelve to twenty-five dollars from each project for making custom draperies, curtains, and quilt tops for the Cadens. She worked for the Caden shop from about 1927 through 1935, later doing alterations for a Lexington department store.

Allie Price (1888–1932) and her husband, Jed, had eight children. He farmed and did carpentry, but during the Depression, farming did not pay "down in the knobs" as Kentuckians call Owsley County in the mountainous

84. Ida Rohrer

85. Allie Turner Price

region north of Hazard. Allie and her daughters quilted for cash. They occasionally received tops in the mail directly from customers, but most of their work came from Ellen Mainous (1880–1965), whose husband had lost his bank in Booneville during the Depression. Like so many other women whose men could not support them, Ellen Mainous turned to sewing. She and her mother and daughter made quilts to order, but her main job was serving as a broker between quilter and customer.

None of the four women who worked on the prize-winning quilt shared the public credit or the $1,000 prize. Mattie Black and Ida Rhorer never made claims to glory or cash. Each felt she could not afford to anger the Cadens with a reminder of her part in the renowned "Quilt of the Century." Louise Rhorer Eddleman recalls her mother's discovery of a newspaper story with the contest results and her immediate recognition of her quilt top as the prize winner. In Ida Rhorer's mind the contest rules had been broken, but "It was Depression times; my father was an invalid, and they had to have their jobs. That was the reason my mother kept her mouth shut."[17]

Helen Black also remembers her mother-in-law's frustration about the injustice, but Mattie Black, grateful for work from the Cadens, felt powerless to complain other than by making jokes within the family. She was a self-effacing woman who did not enter contests and had no need to take credit for the Century of Progress prize winner, although the family would have welcomed extra money.

Allie Price, the quilter, had died by the time the contest winner was announced. Her daughter, Ruth Stewart, remembers hearing that the star they had quilted won a prize, but she had no idea of its enormous value. Another

(continued on page 59)

86. Sample pieces and pattern for the grand prize-winning quilt saved by Mattie Black. The padded quilting of the fern leaves in the green strips elicited the most praise from those who saw the quilt hanging at the fair. Collection of Miriam Tuska.

Kentucky Quilters

The Sears contest was a truly national contest with advertising blanketing the country and final judging sites in ten cities from Seattle to Atlanta. Yet six of the thirty finalists were from Kentucky. (See Appendix for list of names and their hometowns.) The most any other state could boast was two. Geography may have played some part as Kentucky's location allowed its quiltmakers to send quilts to mail-order houses in Memphis, Atlanta, or Chicago. In most states, quilters had only one regional center to which to send their quilts. Yet tripled odds of winning cannot account for the fact that Kentuckians accounted for 20 percent of the finalists.

In an article on cottage industries, quilt historian Cuesta Benberry has called the Kentucky quiltmakers "legendary." She noted that many companies in the early twentieth century boasted of Kentucky needlewomen. The Kentucky connection was, she wrote, "highly advertised and commercialized almost to the point of constituting a Kentucky quiltmakers' mystique."[20]

The authors (adopted and loyal daughters of Tennessee and Kansas, two states where fine quilts are made) acknowledge that the mystique was based on a great deal of truth. Our trip to the state to interview those with information about the prize-winning quilt led us to realize that something was happening in Kentucky during the 1930s, something that had not yet been documented.

88. Ellen Mainous *(second from left)* with her sister-in-law, husband, and daughter, Elberta Botner.

87. Example of the fine professional quilting produced by Kentucky quiltmakers in the 1930s. Collection of Elberta Mainous Botner.

During the time when quilts were often finished for pay, customers made important distinctions between individual professional quilters and groups like the Methodist Ladies' Aid societies who finished tops for a fee to support church building projects and missionary causes. The professional quilters were thought to produce more consistent stitches than the volunteer groups. They were also more likely to do elaborate quilting. The professionals' work was desirable because each quilter, whether she worked alone or with her family, had an individual reputation to build and maintain. Allie Price, credited as the quilter of the grand prize-winning quilt, enjoyed such a reputation. When the Cadens asked Ellen Mainous to find a quilter to do a fast yet skillful job on the Star quilt, she chose Allie Price from among her pool of eighty professional quilters.

89. Ellen Mainous quilting a Grandmother's Flower Garden quilt.

Ellen Mainous's daughter, Elberta Botner, remembers living on the family's 140-acre farm near Levi in Owsley County. During the Depression, when she was in her twenties, her mother acted as an agent for several Kentucky quilt shops and many quiltmakers around the country. She handled up to 1,000 tops per year. Elberta recalled daily trips to the post office to pick up boxes mailed from Lexington and more distant places:

> We kept a map of the United States on a wall in our house. We marked with pins all the states from which we received quilt tops. There's not but two or three states we didn't get quilts from. . . . She never got over fifteen dollars and that would have to be an awful big quilt and quilted real close. She paid [the quilters] nine dollars or ten dollars most of them, maybe some a little more. . . . So if she paid them nine dollars she would keep a dollar or two out; she had to mail them. By the time she took it to the post office she didn't make nothing at all. There was a lot of worry in that work.

Eventually, Ellen Mainous's doctor told her to quit because of the stress, especially the concern over quality. Her daughter also recalled:

> Most of the women did real nice work. They had to . . . to keep quilting. Mother would have everybody bring a sample. Mother'd have to examine their samples. . . . Maybe they did good work and they'd get one out after another one. Sometime's they'd be maybe a month getting one out.[21]

Susie Jackson Combs was another Kentucky quilter whose quilt made it to the Chicago fair. Her Star of France won first prize in the Atlanta regional semifinals and an honorable mention in the national finals. She sold the quilt a few years after the Fair for $250, according to her niece, Reva Crabtree.[22]

Susie Combs, who entered fairs and contests to make a name for herself as a professional quiltmaker, found that winning at the Century of Progress contest provided effective advertising, as it spurred about one hundred orders for quilts. In 1942, *Country Gentleman* added to her prestige and to the mystique of the Kentucky quiltmaker with an article about her thriving business:

> Mrs. Dale Combs of Pebworth, Kentucky, has discovered a secret every woman wants to know: how to sell what you make when everyone around you is making the same things. . . . Like other mountain girls she had learned to quilt quite early but soon was making better quilts than most. The thought of making them for sale was natural when the Depression Thirties brought

(continued)

need for earning a living. All her neighbors had quilts of their own, and a roadside market was out of the question on her untraveled byway. Yet she knew in her bones that if people could only see her work they would buy. Then she had a bright idea. . . . Why not send one of her favorite quilts to the county fair and ask the officials to display it? The quilt traveled alone, for Mrs. Combs could not afford the trip. But it did her proud; it brought back three orders. And that is how, without friends and without fanfare, without capital and without credit, the little business was born. As soon as she heard of another fair, off went the quilt again. Before long her quilts were being exhibited all over the state. The fairs were like a big showcase to her where without cost except for postage and insurance, she could display her wares and attract the attention of people who never would have heard of Mrs. Combs and her fine quilts.[23]

The national prominence of Kentucky quilts and quilters has faded. During the current quilt revival no one area seems to enjoy the prestige Kentucky did in the 1930s. Yet women still make a living from quilting there, and evidence of the state's reputation persists.

Bertha Addison Hensley (born 1922) of Owsley County was invited to the White House to present one of her cooperative projects to first lady Pat Nixon during the 1970s. She has worked for Ellen Mainous, Susie Combs, and many others during her long quilting career. She began quilting with her mother and sisters when she was about ten years old; and when we interviewed her in 1992, she was still quilting one top per week. We asked her how many hours a day she spent quilting:

> Lots of em. Sometimes in there five or six of the morning until midnight. It just depends . . . when I can't sleep, I crawl out and I go to quilting. Nobody bothering me. No phone a-ringing. I just go to town.

90. Bertha Hensley *(third from right)* with members of Save the Children Foundation presenting a Cherry quilt to Mrs. Pat Nixon at the White House.

She can get a quilt out in a week; today she charges from $180 to $850, depending on the amount of quilting. In the early 1930s she remembers earning fifteen dollars.[24]

Did Kentucky quilters have a reputation as the best in the country? We asked Elberta Mainous Botner who replied, "We thought Owsley County did."

(continued from page 55)

daughter, Bess Price Brandenburg, said she remembered Miss Caden winning the prize. Was it fair? "She won the prize. We didn't originate the quilt. . . . There's nothing fair in this world."

Elberta Mainous Botner recalls her mother's reaction when she discovered that the quilt she had handled was the winner:

> It kind of hurt her because she only got ten dollars for it. It made her feel kind of let down or something. She wrote A. M. Caden and said, "I think we deserve a little more because we worked so hard getting this out." If mother had quilted it, it would have took us maybe a month to quilt it and [the Prices] got it out in a couple of weeks or a week and a half. . . . [The Cadens] just never gave her another dime. But it hurt my mother because she worked so hard. I said I'd have liked to have met Mrs. Roosevelt and tell her that my mother worked on that quilt.

Ida Rhorer and Mattie Black kept evidence of their contributions to the Quilt of the Century. Ida Rhorer passed down to her daughter one spare block and scraps of the fabrics from the stars. Mattie Black left pieces of the border fabric with samples of the leaves she stuffed.

Although both Elberta Botner and Ruth Stewart independently attributed the quilting to Allie Price, there is an inconsistency in the story. Allie Price died of tularemia (rabbit fever) in June 1932. To have had a hand in the prize winner, she must have quilted it long before the January 1933 announcement of the Sears contest. It may be the Cadens sent the top with the intention of entering it in another contest and later sent it to the Sears contest. Allie Price may have quilted another diamond star for them. The shop had a repertoire of standard patterns from which customers could choose. The star with the stuffed work might have been ordered frequently before the fair as well as after.

What kind of a woman would refuse to share a large sum of money with four desperately poor women who worked for her? Sarah Caden, widow of Margaret's nephew Tom, whose father was one of the three Caden brothers, remembers Aunt Margaret well.

> She was the prettiest of the sisters, the most delightful one of all six. They were devout Catholics and I was a Protestant. . . . so they didn't accept me very well at first. Later I drove her to our nephew's graduation in Virginia to see him and I would stop every time we'd pass a little Catholic church and . . . let her go in. So, when I got home she said, "If Tom had looked the world over, he couldn't have found a nicer [wife]."

Sarah Caden describes Margaret and Ann Caden as rich. Even during the Depression they profited well from the shop and its branches. Her favorite memory of the aunts is riding the elevator in their large, elegant house. She also recalls some generosity. Once they decided to accept Tom's family, the Caden sisters gave Sarah's daughter Colleen smocked and embroidered dresses from the shop.

When the star quilt was given to Mrs. Eleanor Roosevelt, Margaret Caden was most displeased. Sarah Caden remembers that Margaret did not care for the first lady. "It had nothing to do with politics. She was just disappointed." Margaret Caden commissioned a copy of the stuffed star to replace the prize winner in the White House. She gave the copy to Colleen Caden. Over the years, this quilt, like the Roosevelt quilt, has disappeared.

Women who worked for them described Margaret and Ann Caden as conservative with their money. Elberta Botner recalls that although they initially provided the supplies for quilting,

> the Cadens got so they didn't want to furnish the needles, thread or cotton [batting]. I don't know why. And Mother had to do that and sometimes she'd not earn hardly a dollar on a quilt.

By the time Helen Black entered the Black family in the mid-1940s, "Miss Ann" had died and the shop was closed, but "Miss Margaret" still sold needlework out of her home.

> She still did a little work for the old blue bloods, and Mattie Black was the one that did it. [Mattie Black] was the last one to keep on working. And, oh, Miss Caden was so ugly to her. Oh, it would make me so mad. She would talk rough to her and if she was explaining to Mrs. Black how she wanted something done and Mrs. Black couldn't understand, she would get mad. Now, Ann Caden, who died shortly after I married into the family, was the nice one. And that was the one Mrs. Black liked to deal with because she could understand her, what she wanted and how she wanted it done and all that.

Miss Margaret might have been tight with her money and curt with the help, but was she dishonest enough to deliberately mislead the contest judges? The Cadens' choice to mail their entry to the Sears mail-order house in Chicago rather than to a closer regional mail-order house for the initial judging is provocative. The Cadens may have realized that judges in the southeastern regions would know, to use the words of one of today's Lexington quilters, that "Margaret Caden did not know which end of a needle to thread." The far-away judges at the Chicago mail-order center found the quilt to be the best of the entries shipped to them. It went to the main Sears store in Chicago where it won first prize in its division and on to the fairgrounds where it won Margaret Caden fame and fortune.

"America's Champion Quilter" did not appear to regret her deception. The shop made the most of the advertising opportunity. In January 1934 this advertisement in the *Farmer's Wife* attracted readers' attention:

91. CROWN OF THORNS
also called Rocky Mountain

Maker: Lelia Rawls Porter
Hollins, Alabama, 1933

Pieced: 79″ x 78″; cotton

The quilt pattern was probably copied from an old quilt. Stearns and Foster, Company, adapted the pattern and renamed it New York Beauty in the 1930s.

Collection of the Birmingham Museum of Art; museum purchase with funds from the Fashion Group, Inc., in memory of Mary S. Faust (1985.384).

$1000.00 Prize Quilt at the Century of Progress. The "Star of the Blue Grass" made by Margaret Rogers Caden. Quilt pattern of star and design in stuffed quilting on blocks and border stamped on muslin. To order send $2.00 to A. M. Caden, Lexington, Kentucky. Quilt materials and quilting.

Three years after their World's Fair success, the sisters tried the same formula again. A. M. Caden won an honorable mention at the Eastern States Exposition's national contest with an Eight Point Star characterized in the program as having "effective padded quilting."[18]

The scandal of the Cadens' assembly-line prize winner did not reach the corporate ears of Sears until recent years, although the story has been gossip in Lexington for generations. To place the scandal in the context of the times, it is important to note that Margaret Caden was not the only contestant to cross her fingers as she signed the form stating that her quilt was entirely of her own making. Other finalists like Lois Hobgood Crowell, for instance, had help in sewing and designing. Many finalists purchased kits in which the fabric was marked with cutting lines. Of fourteen entrants answering a questionnaire in the 1970s, five indicated that they had paid other seamstresses to quilt their tops.

92. Lelia Rawls Porter. Photograph courtesy of Birmingham Museum of Art.

Lelia Rawls Porter (1883–1964)

Lelia Rawls Porter was born in Geneva, Alabama, and moved to Hollins as the depot clerk for a railroad. She met her husband, John, there. They had seven children. Her daughter, Marguerite Fulbright, remembers her as a very thrifty person who used her time reading, quilting, and trying all sorts of contests. In 1933, she read about the Sears contest and decided to enter. She bought special fabric for the project and made a pattern. As the contest deadline approached, she became ill, but her Ladies Club came to the house to finish the quilting. Lelia was happy for the help but worried about the inconsistency of the stitches. Her quilt received a green merit award ribbon, but no cash prize.

During the first half of the century, the labor of quiltmaking was commonly divided, with one woman piecing or appliquéing the top and another woman or group of women quilting it. Only in the present quilt revival dating from the 1970s do quiltmakers feel obligated to complete the entire process from choosing fabric, through marking, cutting, sewing, and quilting. Sears contestants who entered quilts finished by church groups or professional quilters may have felt no guilt about signing the entry form because they understood that the quilting was, like much of women's work at the time, considered unimportant and not worth talking about. Certainly, the staff at Sears who wrote the contest rules requiring a statement that the quilt was entirely the work of the entrant had little understanding of the system of shared work then in effect in America's quiltmaking community.

In a 1938 interview for the Federal Writers Project, quiltmaker Dorothy West described late-nineteenth-century attitudes in Charleston about assigning credit.

> Sometimes we'd take our quilts out to the country fairgrounds for exhibition in the fall. Each lady picked out her best quilt—the prettiest color, the prettiest pattern, and the best stitches—and took it to the fair to try to win the prize. It didn't make any difference if your prettiest quilt had been quilted by three or four other people; you already had the pattern and you'd already put the pieces together, so that much was your own idea. And that counted more than the help you got when you were putting it on the frame.[19]

Margaret Caden, however, carried the concept of a cooperative project to extremes that would have been considered immoral even in the era of the professional quilter. Furthermore, no excuses can be made for a woman who did not share the enormous cash prize with the rest of her team. The story of the prize-winning quilt, like so many other stories of quilts made for the fair, cannot be divorced from the Depression when times were hard and women did piecework for pennies. The story of the Caden quilt adds a bittersweet reality to the memories of the Rainbow City and the biggest quilt contest ever held.

FROM TEEPEES TO TEMPLES

The Commemorative Quilts

The authors believe executives of both A Century of Progress and Sears, Roebuck and Company began planning the fair quilt contest with the idea of designating an official Century of Progress quilt. Sears planned to publish designs of the quilts entered in the contest and probably wanted an original World's Fair pattern block to add to its line of quiltmaking items. It reflected this goal in its bonus prize for a commemorative quilt, originally listed as $500 but lowered to $200 by the time the rules were published.

The idea of an official design was forgotten as the contest progressed. However, Leon Harpole, the assistant Sunday editor at the *Chicago Tribune,* remembered the original objective. After reading the contest results, he wrote the fair management:

> I hear that the Sears Roebuck quilt contest has closed, and that no quilt was chosen to bear the title of "A Century of Progress. . . . [May] the *Tribune* originate a design to be known as "A Century of Progress quilt," with the sanction of the Fair administration?[1]

No reply from the fair management exists, but the *Tribune's* quilt columnist, Nancy Cabot, finally published an official Century of Progress pattern on October 22, 1933, which she said was designed "to commemorate Chicago's great pageant in quilt history."[2]

Although Sears did not meet its goal of designating an official quilt, the request for commemorative entries inspired hundreds of American quiltmakers to explore their

93. Detail of Chicago Fair (number 138, page 90)

94. Teepees to Temples, maker unknown, 1933. Photograph courtesy of Sears Archives.

creativity and break from the constraints of commercial patterns. The theme forced quiltmakers to make new decisions about content, design, fabric, and construction.

Linda Rebenstorff, of Stevens Point, Wisconsin, read about the Sears Quilt Contest in her hometown newspaper. The bonus category caught her attention. "They [Sears contest officials] were after the greatest advancements from 1833 to 1933. Conventional quilt designs like Home Star or Flowers would not predict advancement in this century. . . . Why not make a truly historical quilt—one showing some of the changes in the time?" Her husband, Clarence, enjoyed painting and drawing pictures, so she asked him to help with design. His answer was, "I'm with you all the way."

The Rebenstorffs spent six weeks researching in their local library where a librarian became so enthusiastic about their project that she allowed them to take noncirculating reference books home for the weekend. Most of the drawings shown on the quilt's picture blocks are from those library books. The portraits of Thomas Edison, Abraham Lincoln, Franklin D. Roosevelt, and Charles Lindbergh were copied from newspapers and magazines.

The next step was deciding how large to make each block and how to arrange them in an 80″ x 100″ quilt with a three-tone border. They chose Peter Pan gingham for the top and the appliqué, with plain tan percale for the back of the quilt. Clarence shaded the drawings so Linda knew where to put their chosen colors of eggshell, tan, and brown. She transferred the designs to the fabric using carbon paper.

According to the maker, "Edison's face was the hardest to make. He had many wrinkles and a flabby neck. Roosevelt was easy (no wrinkles) and Lindbergh and Lincoln were fairly easy to sew."

The couple hoped to include in each pictorial block the earliest tool and the latest invention for a wide range of technological advancements. For example, the textile industry block contrasts an early 1850s Howe sewing machine with a factory full of 1920s industrial sewing machines operated by young women.

In the borders she embroidered names of dozens of other people who had some impact on the progress of the previous century. These included men and women philanthropists, writers, scientists, and humorists.

According to Linda Rebenstorff, her husband suggested placing a woman as the symbol of progress in the center of the quilt, because "seldom were women given credit for helping man achieve his dreams." Clarence designed a picture of a modern woman holding aloft a platter displaying a torch, a horn of plenty, and an hour glass. The beams of light radiating from the tower of the Sears Building cross with the beams from the woman's torch. According to Linda, the symbolism is, "If you cross the beams of man's inventiveness, progress will keep on going."

Of the fifty-four commemoratives studied for this exhibit, the Rebenstorffs' quilt includes the most complete

(continued on page 69)

95. Clarence and Linda Rebenstorff, 1939

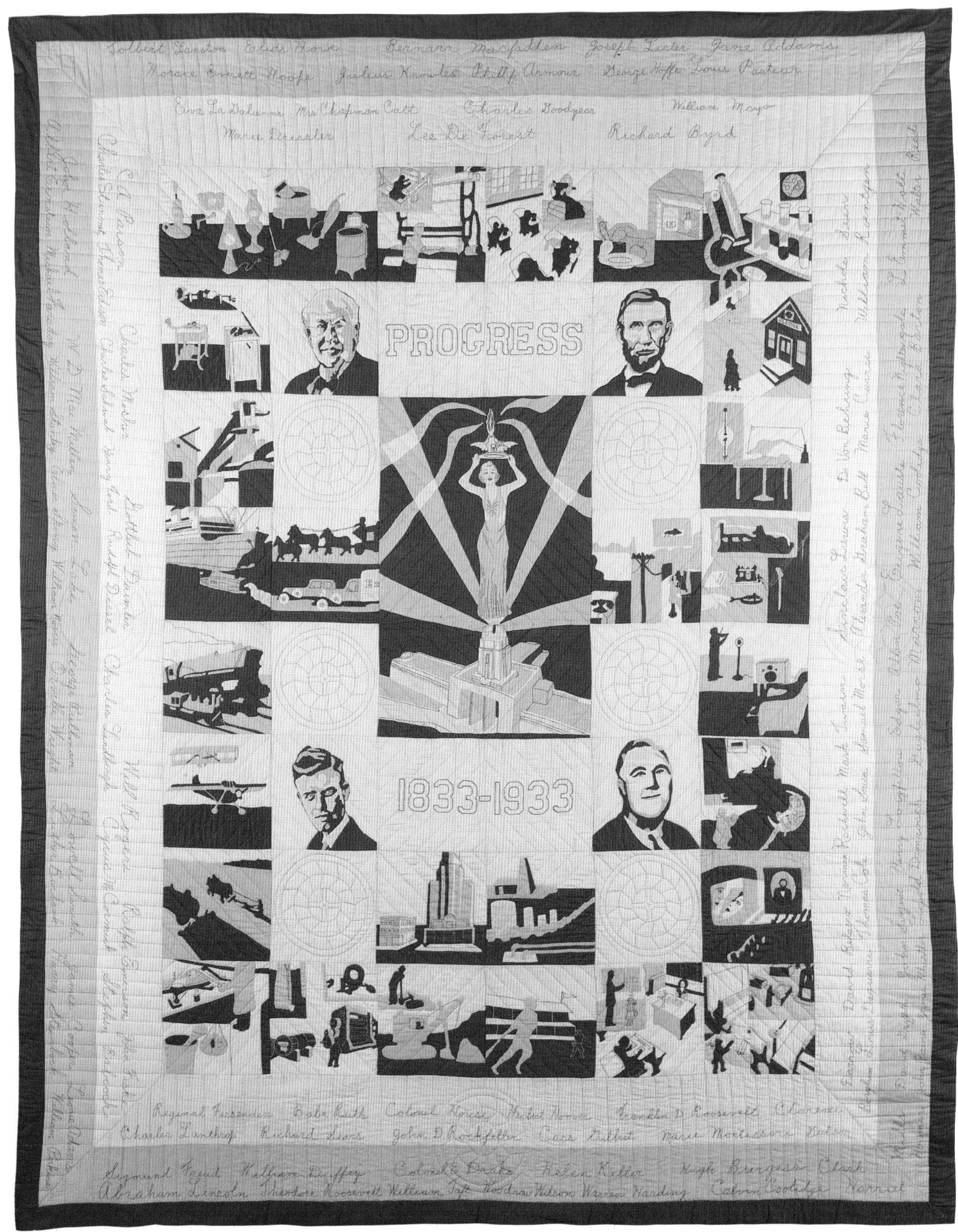

96. THE REBENSTORFF QUILT

Maker: Linda Rebenstorff (1898–1990) and Clarence Rebenstorff (1899–1980)
Caroline, Wisconsin, 1933

Appliquéd: 96″ x 78″; cotton

Collection of Evelyn and Clarence C. Rebenstorff, son.

<table>
<tr><td>Evolution of Lighting: Candles to Electric Lights</td><td>Household Appliances: Hand to Electric</td><td>Hand Loom to Automatic Looms</td><td>Home's first Sewing Machine to Power Machines in Factories</td><td>Refrigeration and Canning</td><td>Bacteriology: Medical Research</td></tr>
<tr><td>Edison's First Phonograph, Later Models and Dictaphone</td><td>Thomas Edison</td><td colspan="2">PROGRESS</td><td>Abraham Lincoln</td><td>Public Health and Welfare</td></tr>
<tr><td>Metalurgy Blast Furnace</td><td>Quilted Turbine Wheel</td><td colspan="2" rowspan="3"></td><td>Quilted Turbine Wheel</td><td>X-Ray Roentgen Tube Therapy Machine</td></tr>
<tr><td>Shipping: Old to Modern</td><td>Pony Express to Autos and Trucks</td><td>Telephone: Bell's First Model, Exchange Desk Model</td><td>Telegraphy: First Model, Later Models</td></tr>
<tr><td>Trains: Old and New Models</td><td>Quilted Turbine Wheel</td><td>Quilted Turbine Wheel</td><td>Radio Communications and Entertainment</td></tr>
<tr><td>Aviation: Wrights' Airplane, Later Model</td><td>Charles Lindbergh</td><td colspan="2">1833—1933</td><td>Franklin D. Roosevelt</td><td>Art Commercialization, Fine Arts, Commercial Art</td></tr>
<tr><td>Rural Machines: Plowing with Horses to Tractors</td><td>Quilted Turbine Wheel</td><td>Architecture: Old and New</td><td>Oil Industry: Col. Drake's First Oil Well; Storage and Modern Transportation</td><td>Quilted Turbine Wheel</td><td>Photography: Daguerreotype to Motion Picture</td></tr>
<tr><td>Research: Scientific</td><td>Rubber Industry: Sap to Vulcanizing, Rolling and Finished Product</td><td>Labor: Hand to Use of Machines</td><td>Sports: Baseball</td><td>Education: No Rods, No Dunce Caps, Better Relationship</td><td>Paper Industry: Rags to Wood Pulp</td></tr>
</table>

97. The maker produced this graph to explain the meaning of each pictorial block in the quilt.

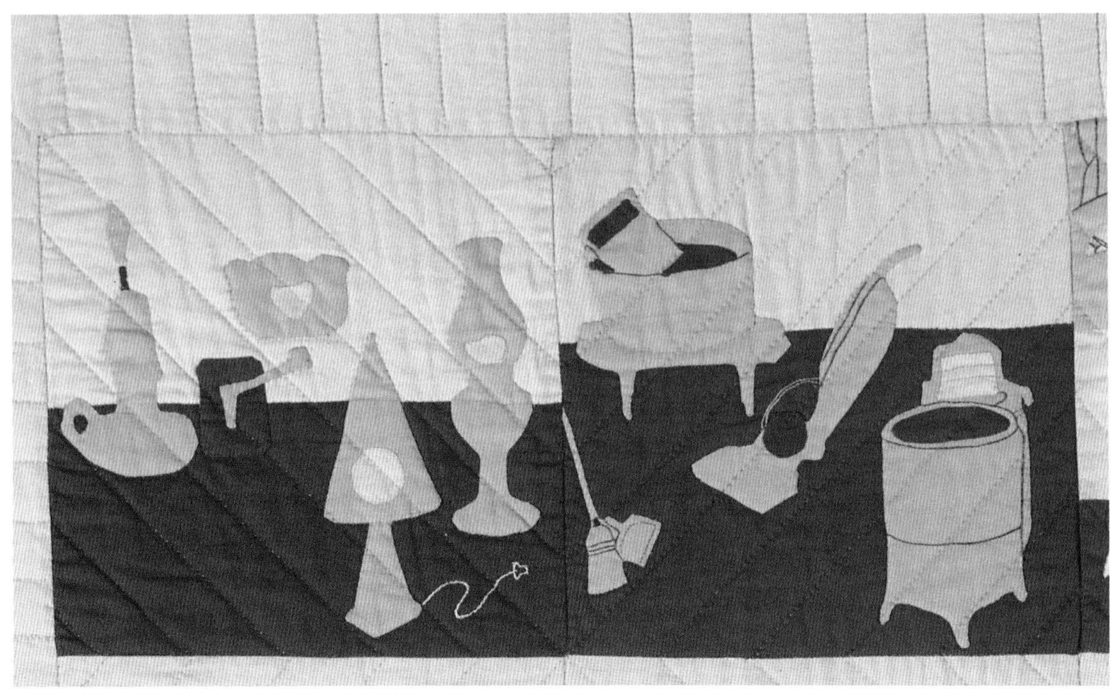

98. Detail of Rebenstorff Quilt showing changes in home appliances.

100. Detail showing Charles Lindbergh, who completed his historic New York to Paris flight in 1927.

99. The designer chose a woman in modern dress and placed her atop the Sears Building to symbolize the contributions women have made to progress.

(continued from page 65)

representation of the changes wrought by the technological advances of the century beginning in 1833. Despite its complexity and skillful technique, it won no prizes. Linda Rebenstorff thought her "poor" quilting might have caused the judges to look at it with disfavor. She reported in a letter that she had finished several of her intricate picture blocks before she realized that original design counted far less than quilting. "I couldn't finish [my quilting], but I sent it to Chicago as is. I knew before I sent it that no prize would it win."

Most quilts did not commemorate the entire range of progress as did the Rebenstorff Quilt. Interpretations of the theme, A Century of Progress, varied. Some merely focused on the dates 1833 and 1933 or the title, "Century of Progress," in quilting, patchwork, or embroidery. Most included appliquéd pictorial images of buildings, inventions, historical scenes, and portraits of inventors and presidents.

Among the group of fifty-four commemorative quilts studied, twenty-one included some aspect of the history of transportation. A few quilts dealt with the impact of progress on social life, especially family life.

Century of Progress quilts made in the Chicago vicinity often depicted Fort Dearborn, the Chicago fire, and the city's modern skyline. Several theme quilts included buildings planned and constructed for the Chicago World's Fair. The Sears Pavilion was a common image since it was pictured in the Sears catalog announcement and the contest entry form. (Certainly, glorifying the contest sponsor's exhibit hall could not hurt one's chances and might indeed help.) Fifteen of the fifty-four quilts contain appliquéd, quilted, or embroidered images of this building.

Some quilts had written messages, such as the Rebenstorffs' list of names of influential people. An unknown maker submitted an album quilt "signed" by important inventors.

Many quilts have more subtle references to the contest theme. Quilting allowed makers to add symbolism in the last step of the quiltmaking process. Lora Montgomery of Fort Wayne, Indiana, quilted a train and several airplanes in the open area surrounding the appliquéd image of the Sears Pavilion. Her border designs included two alternating wheels, a wooden wagon wheel representing transportation in 1833, and a winged rubber tire, symbolizing modern travel. Rose White of Clarkston, Washington, whose quilt won first prize in the Seattle regional contest, chose a traditional pieced star pattern, but quilted the Sears Pavilion, the U.S. Capitol, a victrola, and an airplane in the open areas.

Rose White's quilt was one of two of the thirty finalists that referred to the Century of Progress theme. Mrs. George Leitzel of Northumberland, Pennsylvania, won second prize in the Philadelphia regional contest with an appliquéd representation of progress in transportation. Neither won the $200 bonus prize, which was forgotten in post-fair publicity.

101. Elizabeth Skelly Fitzgerald on her wedding day, November 25, 1937.

Elizabeth Skelly Fitzgerald (1898–1985)

Elizabeth Skelly was a telephone operator and a school cook. When she read about the contest, she took the challenge of creating an original design to commemorate the Century of Progress. She researched transportation and tried to include every available mode of transportation. She sent her quilt to the Philadelphia mail-order center for judging, but this striking quilt did not win a prize.

102. TRANSPORTATION QUILT

Maker: Elizabeth Skelly Fitzgerald
Highland Falls, New York, 1933

Pieced and appliquéd with embroidery: 82″ x 69½″; cotton

Collection of Charles Fitzgerald and Margaret McDonald, son and daughter.

103. The appliqué layering of the motorcycle's features is a delight to behold.

SEARS, ROEBUCK and CO.

Regional Prize-Winning Quilts in Great National Quilting Contest

THE THREE QUILTS ARE FIRST THREE PRIZE WINNERS

CENTURY-PROGRESS QUILTING CONTEST

THESE THREE QUILTS

CHICAGO STORE

NATIONAL CONTEST

FIRST NATIONAL PRIZE $1000

Pictured above are the quilts which were awarded, last Thursday, the three regional prizes in Sears Much-Talked-Of National Quilting Contest. The names of the lucky quilters are to be found in the story to the right. Lower left: Judging the contest were Mrs. William E. Lingelbach, president of the Philadelphia Federation of Women's Clubs; Caroline B. King, Women's Editor of The Country Gentleman, and Mr. Bernard Davis, president of La France Industries. Beautiful and intricate were the hundreds of designs, evidencing many, many hours of tedious labor on the part of the contestant quilt-makers.

104. Results of the Philadelphia regional contest show the only pictorial commemorative quilt included in the final-round judging in Chicago at the Sears Building. Mrs. George Leitzel of Northumberland created the quilt that depicts progress in transportation. Also pictured are Sunburst by Mrs. Virgil Carpenter of Hyndman, Pennsylvania, and Autumn Leaves by Mrs. Edith Snyder of Buffalo, New York. Collection of H. M. Carpenter.

Several of the commemoratives were designed as works of art, with the artists preparing watercolors before beginning quilt construction. Such a design process, as well as the use of pictorial, symbolic, and abstract design not drawn from traditional quilt patterns, characterizes the makers as artists working before their time. In 1933 their works were treated as curiosities. Only now, decades after the contest, contemporary emphasis on creativity, originality, and nontraditional textile arts affords the commemoratives the appreciation they have so long deserved.

The absence of official attention was a loss not only to the artists who worked hard in the spring of 1933, but also to the greater quiltmaking community. If the commemoratives had received more acclaim, they might have challenged American needlewomen to reach beyond the commercial patterns available to them. The results of the Sears contest might have been the flowering of an innovative quilt style during the Depression years, rather than a confirmation of the paint-by-number approach encouraged by the pattern companies.

The judges' decision to ignore nontraditional quilts cooled creativity, stole dreams, and raised a few tempers. Ida Stow expressed her indignation by withdrawing her commemorative quilt from the display after the midwestern regional judging at the main Chicago store. She wrote to Sears of her disgust:

> Many of we exhibitors spent considerable time, thought and energy not to speak of money, in our efforts to produce something worthwhile along the lines called

105. Detail of Sears Pavilion Quilt (number 32, page 18). For the borders, the maker developed a clever design of wagon wheels and balloon tires with a wing (a familiar advertising logo in 1933) to depict the Century of Progress in road transportation.

106. Tempera drawing of quiltmaker's design for Century of Progress combined with World Without End. See number 1, page ii, and cover.

107. Commemorative quilts on display at the Sears Pavilion in summer 1934. Photograph courtesy of Sears Archives.

> for by your company, to produce "an unusual design to depict and commemorate the Century of Progress" and it is not with justice to us or your reputation to have the matter handled in this manner. Will you kindly give this your consideration and see if this quilt contest can be handled with fairness and along the lines originally laid down by you.[3]

Such criticism may have inspired Sears to mount a small exhibit devoted to commemoratives during the fair's second season. That year Sears photographers documented the quilts on view, recording both the ten finalists and the display of commemoratives. The photographs have been in Sears archives for decades, but the designers of the commemoratives were not recorded and the quilts' current locations also are unknown.

Sixty years late, we present in the next few pages the second exhibit of the commemorative quilts, offering a broad interpretation of the theme of the fair. Chicago's historic past, the country's technological advances, Sears, Roebuck and Company's presence, and the fair itself are stitched, appliquéd, and embroidered into these special twentieth-century quilts.

A Gallery of Commemoratives

Historic USA

Fanny and Charles Normann, a Texas couple, collaborated on their Sears contest entry. The quilt in silk appliqué is a reproduction of an oil painting of the signing of the Declaration of Independence. Surrounding the scene is an oval with the faces of all the American presidents up to 1933. George Washington and Abraham Lincoln are in larger ovals at the top and bottom. President Roosevelt appears just under the likeness of George Washington. In the quilt corners are other American symbols: the Liberty Bell, an eagle with outspread wings, and the Statue of Liberty.

In 1986 Fanny Normann wrote to Karey Bresenhan, a noted Texas quilt authority, asking for advice on the care of her prized quilt. In the letter, she explained with pride the circumstances under which her Century of Progress quilt was made:

> We married in '28—just prior to the drop-out depression—while Mr. Normann was teaching art and doing reproductions at Bradford Paint Company on Ninth and Colorado in Austin. He was a sensitive, experimental traveler, trying to become quickly American after hav-

108. HISTORIC USA

Makers: Fanny and Charles Normann
Texas, 1933

Pieced and appliqué with embroidery: 93″ x 75″; cotton

Collection of Artie Fultz Davis. Photograph courtesy of the Star of the Republic Museum in Washington, Texas.

109. Newly elected Franklin D. Roosevelt is included inside the ring of U.S. presidents.

110. Charles Normann made a living painting reproductions of oil paintings. For this undertaking, he worked in silk.

ing arrived in Minnesota in '22, at age 19, from Norway. He was making his way on a day-to-day basis with an extreme proficiency in fine art. He sometimes managed to do as many as three Old Master's reproductions in a day at three dollars each, for which [his employer] might easily obtain fifty dollars each. Yet nine dollars a day . . . was a better than average wage in '28.

Suffice us to say, however, that this rate didn't last after the bottom dropped. When Sears offered $1,000 first prize for best quilt at Chicago's Exposition, we hopped-to with a determination to win that, regardless! Mr. Normann put his best expertise to work on a design and procedure, and we stitched away, eighteen hours a day for three months, by the light of a kerosene lamp after the sun went down—the two of us at my father's farm in Burnet County, with a baby daughter to care for on the side. At last, we had finished! Just six weeks after FDR's first inaugural.

There were always friends to brighten the occasions. This time, Tony Kutalek, builder of fine furnishings for the elite of Austin, insisted that we bring the quilt down at the first possible moment and let Austin see it. We must conquer Austin first, high style! Even Governor Miriam A. Ferguson was invited to the showing at Kutalek's home . . . and the *Statesman* reporter dared to say this could be the New Deal that could make it for Artist Normann—with young wife and eleven-month-old daughter. We had to win! But we didn't. Somehow our quilt was barred from entering the contest we'd made it for—maybe because Sears and Company had other than fine art in mind when they offered the prize to their customers.

From 1833 to 1933

While the Normann's Historic USA focused on a significant event in America's history and the Rebenstorff Quilt documented technological changes, the quilt made by Emma Mae Leonhard of Virginia, Illinois, incorporated social changes during the previous century.

In a typed statement, Emma Mae Leonhard explained her quilt's message. Like many other quilters, she featured changes in transportation. The border contains covered wagons of the 1800s, steam engines on railroads, covered trucks and luxurious automobiles on the highway of 1933, and finally the air space conquered by Charles Lindbergh and his *Spirit of St. Louis*.

The original pieced block repeated nine times has a simple, rustic cabin at the base while towering over it are skyscrapers. This block depicts Chicago's development from a settlement of simple log cabins to a major city of skyscrapers in brick, steel, and glass.

Alternating with the pieced blocks are eight appliqué blocks that document changes in women's fashions. The 1833 figure wears a simple dress with leg o'mutton sleeves, bonnet, and crinolines, while the 1933 figure wears a low-cut dress with a slender skirt.

Across the bottom of the quilt is a block Emma Mae called the "War Block." Appliqué figures represent the four wars the nation had fought during the previous century: the Mexican War, the Civil War, the Spanish-American War, and the Great War (later known as World War I). Two figures represent a battlefield nurse and a homefront volunteer. A Palm of Peace hovers over the Tomb of the Unknown Soldier.

At the top of the quilt, the maker highlighted changes in horticulture. In 1833 the wild rose was the national flower; by 1933 the hybrid rose looked very different. Both types are appliquéd on her quilt.

In the four corners, appliquéd figures carrying American flags represent the Boy Scouts (founded in 1910), the Sea Scouts (1931), the Girl Scouts (1912), and the Camp Fire Girls (1911).

Emma Mae Leonhard used her quilting designs to expand on the theme A Century of Progress. A palm representing Christianity and an eagle representing democracy are quilted into the side areas. The Statue of Liberty was included so that "we not forget the services that the immigrant has given to us, as well as the happiness our nation has furnished the immigrant."

In the plain block at the left, she focused on the importance of Native Americans in the development of the United States. Quilted into the surface of the quilt are an Indian, Santos of the Avaripa Apaches, shaking hands

111. Emma Mae Leonhard

Emma Mae Leonhard (1890–1976)

Emma Mae Leonhard grew up with seven brothers and sisters in Virginia, Illinois. She graduated from Illinois College in Jacksonville and taught high school English there for forty-five years. Her lifetime hobbies and interests are expressed in the varied motifs of her Century of Progress quilt. She was involved in the Camp Fire Girls organization and served as a Red Cross volunteer during World War I. In her later years she led birding expeditions to various places in the United States and served as president of the Audubon Society of Illinois. A wildlife sanctuary by the lake at Jacksonville is named in her honor.

112. FROM 1833 TO 1933

Maker: Emma Mae Leonhard
Virginia, Illinois, 1933

Pieced and appliqué: 84½″ x 75″; cotton sateen

Collection of Ardis and Robert James.

113. Santos of the Avaripa Apaches shakes hands with General Howard.

114. An original pieced block depicts Chicago's growth from a log settlement to a skyscraper city.

with General Howard, an officer in the Civil War and later an ambassador to the Indians. According to the quilt-maker, Santos was the first Indian who consented to go to Washington, D.C., to talk with government leaders. In addition to his work with Native Americans, General Howard was instrumental in establishing Howard University, an institution of higher learning dedicated to educating African-Americans. He also founded Lincoln Memorial University for mountain whites.

In 1933 Emma Mae Leonhard was a high school English teacher and an early environmentalist. This quilt and her accompanying explanation are a tribute to a teacher's desire to look for the positive and communicate it to others. She reminds the viewer that true progress, as great as inventions and discoveries might be, is based on sacrifice, service, and concern for the world.[4]

115. The 1933 figure shows a modern young woman in slenderizing dress.

116. The 1833 figure shows a woman in a simple dress with crinolines and bonnet.

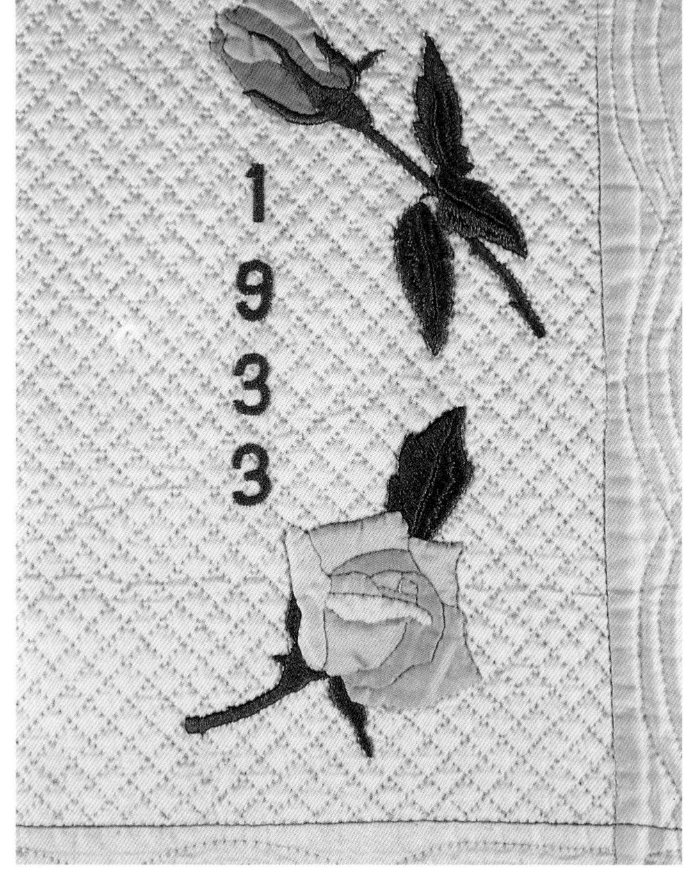

117. This block features the rose cultivated to 1933 standards.

The Album of Inventors

Unfortunately, not all the Century of Progress quilts were as well documented as the previous two. This quilt slipped into the antiques market and the maker's name has been lost. The authors have named it An Album of Inventors. In the border the maker used a traditional quilt block called Album, often found in Friendship quilts of the mid-1800s. If a family was moving to another part of the country, friends and relatives would write their names in the white space in the center of the block. Sometimes they would add short messages of friendship such as, "When this you see, think of me."

The quiltmaker, by embroidering the names of eighteen famous people whose inventions had shaped the industrial progress of America up to 1933, performed a similar service by memorializing the people and their accomplishments.

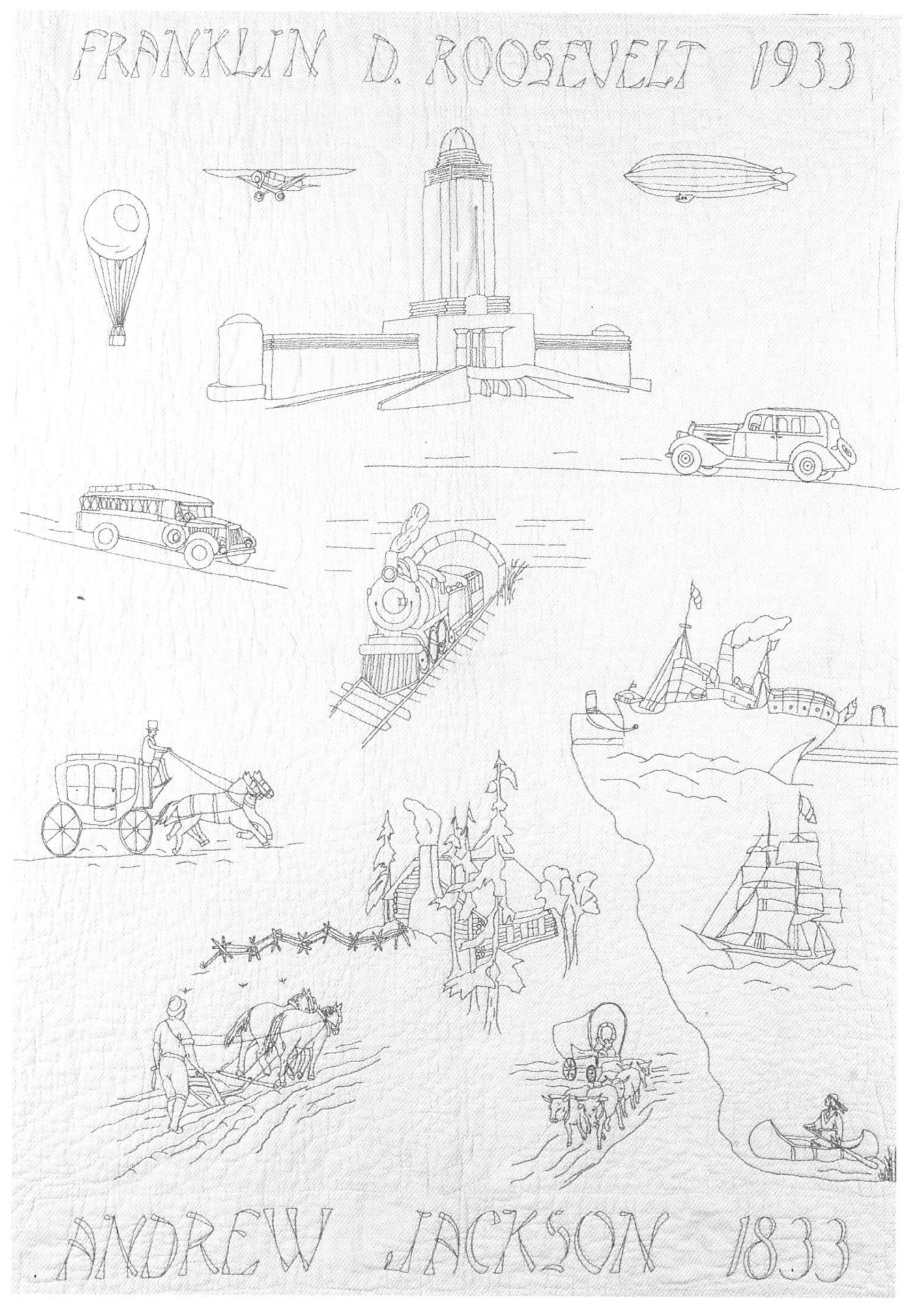

118. Detail of Album of Inventors shows progress from 1833 to 1933.

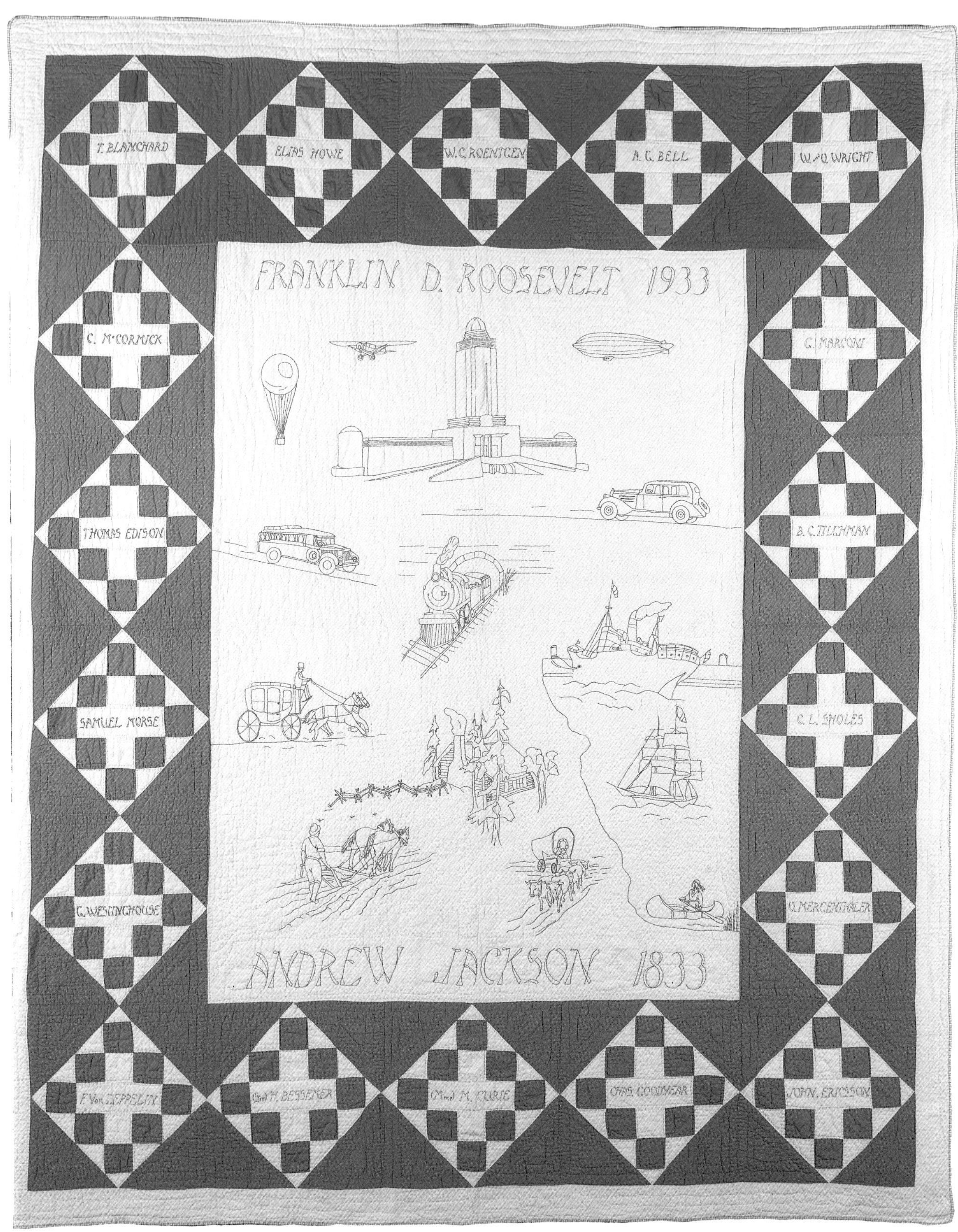

119. ALBUM OF INVENTORS

Maker: Unknown
1933

Pieced and embroidered: 89″ x 72″; cotton

Collection of Shelly Zegart.

In the large white central area, the quilter arranged a pictorial narrative vertically. Across the top is embroidered the name of the newly elected president in 1933, Franklin D. Roosevelt. Across the bottom is the name of the president in 1833, Andrew Jackson. Between the two presidents' names are scenes depicting changes in the American life and landscape. The maker probably found the scenes in books and magazines, traced them, enlarged them if needed, and then transferred them to the quilt's surface.

At the bottom, an Indian travels by canoe, a farmer plows with horses, and families move by covered wagon. Soon the stagecoach, train, then a bus transport people more efficiently and comfortably. At the top, an automobile heads to the 1933 Century of Progress Exposition represented by the Sears Pavilion, a familiar building included in these Century of Progress quilts.

I Will Quilt

Another Century of Progress quilt, whose maker is also unknown, is easy to decipher after one has studied Chicago history and the city's world's fairs. The authors have named this quilt I Will because of the appliqué likeness of the "I Will" lady embroidered in the center oval of the quilt. She represents the city's fierce determination in the 1800s to overcome all obstacles and emerge as a first-class world city.

The four intricately appliquéd scenes of this silk quilt are dated and each represents an important event in Chicago history. In the upper left corner, the 1673 scene shows a traveler, probably French explorer Father Marquette or Louis Joliet, making his way by canoe through the swampy area known by the Indians as "Checagou." In the upper right corner, Fort Dearborn has been erected by the U.S.

The inventors' names beginning in the upper right corner and proceeding clockwise are: Wilbur and Orville Wright (1867–1912) and (1871–1948), American inventors of the system of control used in flying machines today; Guglielmo Marconi (1874–1937), Italian physicist known for his work on the wireless telegraph; Richard Albert Tilghman (1824–1899), American chemist who developed processes for manufacturing paper pulp and producing gas from coal; Christopher Latham Sholes (1819–1890), American publisher who patented a paging machine, a numbering machine, and the first industrial typewriter; Ottmar Mergenthaler (1854–1899), German-born American inventor of linotype; John Ericsson (1803–1889), American naval engineer and builder of the *Monitor;* Charles Goodyear (1800–1860), American inventor of the sulphur vulcanizing process for rubber; Marie Sklodowska Curie (1867–1934), Polish-born French chemist and physicist who discovered radium and polonium in collaboration with her husband, Pierre; Sir Henry Bessemer (1813–1898), English engineer and inventor of a steel manufacturing process named after him; Count Ferdinand von Zeppelin (1838–1917), German general and inventor of the aluminum frame dirigible balloon; George Westinghouse (1846–1914), American inventor of the air brake, a device for replacing derailed steam cars, and distribution systems for electricity and natural gas; Samuel Morse (1791–1872), American inventor of the telegraph and the sending and receiving apparatus known as Morse Code; Thomas Edison (1847–1931), American patenter of more than 1,300 inventions including the incandescent lamp, phonograph, and microphone; Cyrus McCormick (1809–1884), American inventor of farming implements including a threshing machine; Thomas Blanchard (1788–1864), toolmaker and inventor of a tack machine, a steam wagon, a steam boat that could go upstream, and a heavy timber-bending process; Elias Howe (1819–1867), American inventor of the sewing machine; Wilhelm Roentgen (1845–1923), German physicist and discoverer of X-rays; and Alexander Graham Bell (1847–1922), American inventor of the telephone plus flat and cylindrical wax records for phonographs.

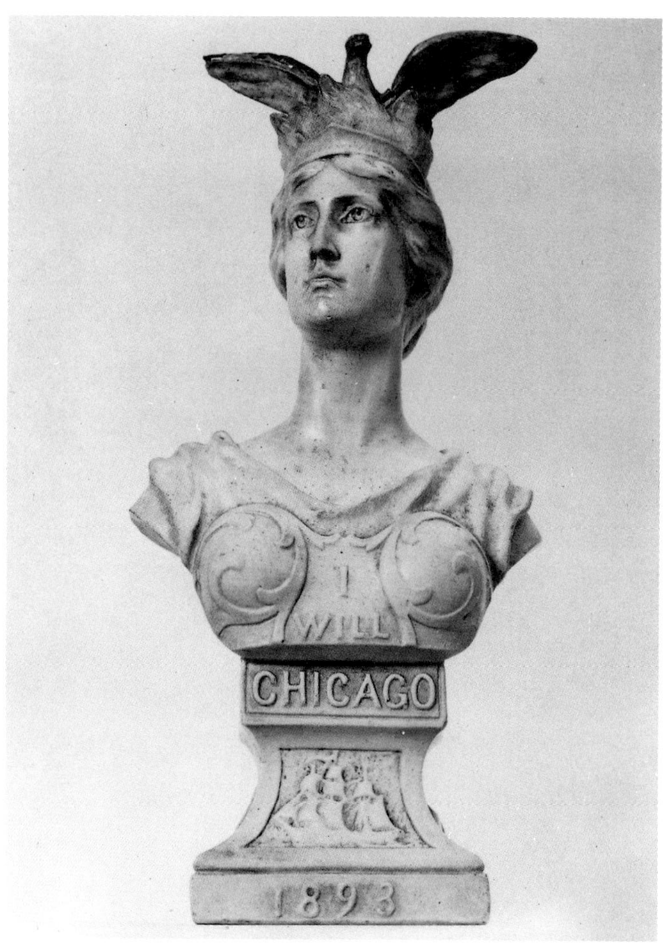

120. The souvenir bust of "I Will" designed for the 1893 Columbian Exposition by Charles Holloway, a Chicago artist, became the city's symbol of civic spirit. Photograph courtesy of the Chicago Historical Society.

121. I WILL

Maker: Unknown
Possibly made in Iowa or Illinois, 1933

Pieced and appliqué and embroidered: 89″ x 75″; silk

Collection of Marilyn M. Woodin and Kalona Quilt and Textile Museum, Kalona, Iowa.

122. Detail of I Will showing a seventeenth-century explorer.

123. Detail of I Will showing 1803 Fort Dearborn.

government in 1803. In the lower left corner, the flames of the famous 1871 fire devour the city's buildings. In the bottom right corner, Chicago is depicted in 1933, on its one-hundredth birthday, as a vital city with sailboats arriving at its lake front and airplanes flying overhead.

The appliqué woman in the center is based on a figure drawn by a famous Chicago artist for an 1892 contest sponsored by *Inter-Ocean,* a Chicago newspaper. The newspaper was looking for a figure who would convey the character of the city, which had risen from the destruction of the 1871 fire and persevered in its drive to host the 1893 World's Columbian Exposition. Charles Holloway, a prominent Chicago artist, won first prize. His I Will lady in her classic garb and phoenix headdress became a familiar figure in sculpture and drawings at the 1893 Columbian World's Exposition. In this quilt she serves as the link between the 1893 fair and the 1933 fair.

Surrounding the I Will figure are symbols of the 1933 Century of Progress Exposition. The fair's logo of a spinning Arcturus star appears twice in appliqué. The same spinning star motifs are also quilted into the purple border. The quilt is dated 1933 in appliqué numerals, and a small flag declares this fair to be the one-hundredth anniversary of the city of Chicago.

Although the present owner does not know who made the quilt or the circumstances under which it was made, the quilt contains more than enough information to link it to the Century of Progress quilt contest.

124. The I Will lady forming the center medallion commemorates the spirit of Chicago and links the 1933 World's Fair to the earlier 1893 fair. Photograph courtesy of the Chicago Historical Society.

Fort Dearborn Quilt

At the site of present-day Chicago, a log cabin had been built by Jean Baptiste du Sable, an African-American from Santo Domingo, who was the city's first non-native resident. This cabin was purchased in 1804 by John Kinzie. Fort Dearborn was established by the U.S. government in 1803 on the south bank of the Chicago River on land where Michigan Avenue is today. However, in August 1812 the soldiers were ordered to retreat from the fort. Indians killed the retreating soldiers and burned Fort Dearborn to the ground.

A replica of Fort Dearborn was one of the first attractions erected on the fair site, and for several months before the fair actually opened Chicagoans were invited to tour the fort for a small admission charge. This may have been why Fort Dearborn appears so often in the Century of Progress commemorative quilts. In our collection of fifty-four commemorative quilts, Fort Dearborn is included eight times.

CHICAGO SUNDAY TRIBUNE May 8, 1949 Part 3—Page

Puts Fort Dearborn on a Quilt

Mrs. Mary Fitzgerald, 1211 E. 72d st., displays her Fort Dearborn quilt, so called because of the picture of the historic fort appliqued in the middle of it. The seamstress is 83 years old and believes she has made about 100 quilts since she first learned the craft at the age of 12. (TRIBUNE Photo)

WIDOW, 83, SOWS SEEDS OF ART IN FANCY SEWING

An artist with a needle for a brush and a quilting frame for a

125. 1949 *Chicago Tribune* article about Mary Fitzgerald and her quilt described by the reporter as "a mural in symbolism."

Fort Dearborn, the Kinzies' log cabin, and the Indians are depicted in a quilt made by sixty-seven-year-old Mary Fitzgerald of Chicago. Although her quilt did not win an award in the 1933 contest, it received widespread coverage when it was described by the maker in a 1949 article in the *Chicago Tribune*. In an accompanying photo, she was shown with her quilt which the newspaper described as "a mural in symbolism."

126. Mary O'Halloran Fitzgerald

Mary O'Halloran Fitzgerald (1866–1957)

Mary O'Halloran was educated at a convent school in Rensselaer, Indiana. There she learned quilting, lace making, crewel, and needlepoint. After schooling, she took a job as a nanny. While walking her charges in a park, she met a young police officer, Thomas Fitzgerald. They were married in 1892 and had three children of their own.

In 1924 Mary Fitzgerald won a major contest in Aurora, Illinois, with an appliqué quilt. Her Sears contest entry, Fort Dearborn, won a green ribbon of honorable mention at a Chicago store, but it was not among the finalists shown at the fair. Following the fair, she promoted quiltmaking by organizing quilting clubs in the Chicago area and lecturing about quilts.

127. FORT DEARBORN

Maker: Mary O'Halloran Fitzgerald
Chicago, Illinois, 1933

Appliquéd and embroidered: 80″ x 80″; cotton

Collection of Ann Reiser, great-granddaughter, and Alice Katzmarek, granddaughter.

128. Mrs. Kinzie waits in front of her cabin as a battle brews outside Fort Dearborn.

129. The layering of the small strips of fabric creates a realistic log building.

130. Admission ticket to the 1933 fair and an admission ticket to Fort Dearborn and the Lama Temple, popular attractions at the Century of Progress.

131. Replica of Fort Dearborn at A Century of Progress.

Scenes from Early America

Fort Dearborn also appears in the center of the Scenes from Early America quilt made by Thelma Burleigh Johnston. Surrounding the Fort are richly detailed appliqué scenes depicting nostalgic views of transportation, domestic arts, housing, and clothing. The maker won a green ribbon of honorable mention for the quilt, but she did not receive a cash prize.

133. Thelma Burleigh Johnston, 1928

132. The maker traced nostalgic scenes from pictures she found in coloring books and magazines and then rendered them in intricate appliqué.

134. Print fabrics used in the appliqué are mostly reproductions of nineteenth-century fabrics. The appliqué scenes are repeated in the quilting designs of the plain white blocks.

135. The Tudor-style home contrasts with the log cabin.

136. SCENES FROM EARLY AMERICA

Maker: Thelma Burleigh Johnston
Long Lake, Minnesota, 1933

Appliqué: 82″ x 68″; cotton

The quilt won honorable mention and received a green merit award ribbon, but the family is not sure if the quilt was entered in the Minneapolis contest.

Collection of Evelyn Crittenden, niece.

Thelma Burleigh Johnston (1908–1982)

Thelma Burleigh Johnston was one of the original 99ers, an organization of woman aviators. In photograph 133 (page 87), taken in 1928, Thelma was employed as a housemaid. Every day at 5:00 A.M. she would walk to the airfield for her early morning flying lessons. She later married and raised four children. Her husband kept up a small farm while working at odd jobs in the community. At the time of the contest, they were renting a cottage on the shores of Long Lake, Minnesota.

The Chicago Fair Quilt

This quilt features historic episodes in the development of Bertha Stenge's home city. Indian teepees, Fort Dearborn, the great fire—all common images in other commemorative quilts—fill the bottom half of the central medallion while modern skyscrapers, a freighter, and a modern building from the Century of Progress Exposition fill the top portion.

Ten years after the close of the fair, the quilt was featured in a *Christian Science Monitor* article about the quiltmaker. The reporter did not identify the modern edifice as the Travel and Transport Building, which was destroyed after the fair, with its fame probably quickly dissipating.

This building appeared in five of the commemorative quilts studied, proof that the hall was completed months before the fair opened and that it had already become a symbol of the 1933 Century of Progress. Designed by architects Edward Bennett, Hubert Burnham, and John Holabird, the Travel and Transport Building set the standard for the architectural gems the fair officials hoped for. The circular building featured exposed columns which supported the floating roof, thus requiring no interior columns to obstruct the large exhibit space. Unfortunately, not all the other Fair pavilions were as innovative.

137. Bertha Stenge

Bertha Stenge (1891–1957)

Bertha Stenge and her husband, Bernhard, an attorney, met in her native state of California but moved to Chicago in 1920 to settle and raise a family. Bertha had studied stained-glass window-making in California.

In 1930 Bertha Stenge made her first quilt from the Nancy Page Alphabet Quilt series pattern. At the same time, her young daughters worked on their own quilts made of the same pattern. All the quilts were entered in a contest sponsored by a Chicago newspaper, but none of the Stenge women won.

In May 1933, Bertha entered a commemorative quilt in the Sears Quilt Contest. The same month the contest announcement came out, she wrote a touching letter to *Woman's Home Companion* which appeared in July 1933:

> Dear Editor: I became acquainted with your magazine while still a school girl in a small town. All this time I have watched you put on weight and gain prestige. As a girl I was called an artist and earned a penny now and then. Then came love and marriage and children. Now at the age of 42, my youngsters need me only to hold the reins in check. A maid relieves me of the heavy household tasks and I'm lost.
>
> I try to make my own designs, but after twenty-two years it is the hardest kind of work instead of the simple joy designing used to be.
>
> Won't you broadcast to your readers that they profit by my mistake and take time out, if not daily, at least weekly to keep in touch with their talents. When the time comes that they find themselves unnecessary to the welfare of the family, they can easily slip into other joyful work and not become superfluous, a neurotic, a prying mother-in-law or a member of the gossipers' course.
>
> It's the 42-year-old mother's lament that the children don't need you anymore and you still have time to fill.
>
> B. S. Illinois

The original design, Chicago Fair, created for the 1933 contest, was the first of many original designs she created, but it did not win a prize.

In 1940 she won first place for her Palm Leaf Hosannah quilt in the New York World's Fair Quilt Contest called "America through the Needle's Eye." In 1942, she won the $1,000 Grand Prize in *Woman's Day* Magazine's National Needlework Contest for her quilt Victory.

In 1941, she was invited to show her quilts at the Art Museum at the University of California at Berkeley. In 1943, an exhibit of seventeen of her quilts opened at the Art Institute of Chicago.

She continued to enter her quilts in competitions throughout the United States and Canada. Obviously, through her quiltmaking she rediscovered the "simple joy designing once was."

Information provided by family of Bertha Stenge, Frances Traynor, Prudence Fuchsman, Milton Wishnick, Carolyn Golden, and Jean Wishnick.

138. CHICAGO FAIR

Maker: Bertha Stenge
Chicago, Illinois, 1933

Pieced and appliquéd: 76″ x 76″; cotton

Collection of the Chicago Historical Society. Photograph courtesy of the Chicago Historical Society.

Sears Pavilion

Of all the attractions at the 1933 fair, the Sears Pavilion appears most often in the commemorative quilts. Of the fifty-four commemorative quilts studied, fifteen contain an illustration of this building. Since its image had appeared in the Sears catalog and the contest informational flier, quiltmakers could simply draw or trace it and transfer it to cloth in embroidery or appliqué or a combination of the two. At least three quilts used the Sears Pavilion as the central feature of the quilt.

A quilt entered by Anna Hansen of Chicago had as its central motif an illustration of the Sears Pavilion rendered by her husband. The source of his design is undoubtedly the contest flier which contained the same drawing. The quiltmaker has added flying machines above the building and the words "Century of Progress, Chicago, June 1933."

Other quiltmakers simply incorporated the Sears Pavilion inconspicuously in the overall design. The maker of the quilt called the Clipper Ship has an intricately appliquéd and embroidered five-inch-wide image of the building in the border at the bottom of the quilt.

139. Detail of number 3, page xv. The Sears Building is intricately executed in this appliqué motif.

140. CENTURY OF PROGRESS

Maker: Anna Hansen
Chicago, Illinois, 1933

Appliqué and pieced: 84″ x 72″; cotton

This quilt is dated June 1933, the month the fair was scheduled to open; however, the opening date was moved up to May 28, 1933, to accommodate the schedule of President Roosevelt.

Collection of LeRoy and Maxine Armstrong.

The final quilt, another masterpiece of design and execution, also unfortunately has an unknown maker. The appliqué scenes remind the viewer that the travel advances of the previous century are no longer daydreams. The rising sun behind the Sears Building welcomes a new day full of promises for progress. Facing one of the most desperate economic times in their history, visitors to this quilt exhibit might have been wishing for more of the past and less of the present.

141. CENTURY OF PROGRESS

Maker: Unknown
1933

Appliqué: 88½″ x 77½″; cotton

Collection of Marilyn Forbes.

This commemorative quilt features the most frequently used elements of the Century of Progress quilts: the Sears Pavilion and the theme of advances in travel.

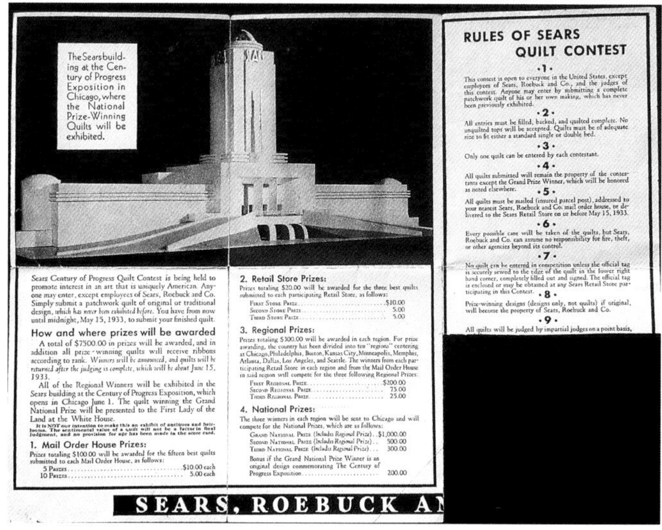

The Sears building at the Century of Progress Exposition in Chicago, where the National Prize-Winning Quilts will be exhibited.

Sears Century of Progress Quilt Contest is being held to promote interest in an art that is uniquely American. Anyone may enter, except employees of Sears, Roebuck and Co. Simply submit a patchwork quilt of original or traditional design, *which has never been exhibited before*. You have from now until midnight, May 15, 1933, to submit your finished quilt.

How and where prizes will be awarded

A total of $7500.00 in prizes will be awarded, and in addition all prize-winning quilts will receive ribbons according to rank. *Winners will be announced, and quilts will be returned after the judging is complete, which will be about June 15, 1933.*

All of the Regional Winners will be exhibited in the Sears building at the Century of Progress Exposition, which opens in Chicago June 1. The quilt winning the Grand National Prize will be presented to the First Lady of the Land at the White House.

It is NOT our intention to make this an exhibit of antiques and heirlooms. The sentimental value of a quilt will not be a factor in final judgment, and no provision for age has been made in the score card.

1. Mail Order House Prizes:

Prizes totaling $100.00 will be awarded for the fifteen best quilts submitted to each Mail Order House, as follows:

5 Prizes	$10.00 each
10 Prizes	5.00 each

2. Retail Store Prizes:

Prizes totaling $20.00 will be awarded for the three best quilts submitted to each participating Retail Store, as follows:

First Store Prize	$10.00
Second Store Prize	5.00
Third Store Prize	5.00

3. Regional Prizes:

Prizes totaling $300.00 will be awarded in each region. For prize awarding, the country has been divided into ten "regions" centering at Chicago, Philadelphia, Boston, Kansas City, Minneapolis, Memphis, Atlanta, Dallas, Los Angeles, and Seattle. The winners from each participating Retail Store in each region and from the Mail Order House in said region will compete for the three following Regional Prizes:

First Regional Prize	$200.00
Second Regional Prize	75.00
Third Regional Prize	25.00

4. National Prizes:

The three winners in each region will be sent to Chicago and will compete for the National Prizes, which are as follows:

Grand National Prize (*Includes Regional Prize*)	$1,000.00
Second National Prize (*Includes Regional Prize*)	500.00
Third National Prize (*Includes Regional Prize*)	300.00
Bonus if the Grand National Prize Winner is an original design commemorating The Century of Progress Exposition	200.00

RULES OF SEARS QUILT CONTEST

•1•

This contest is open to everyone in the United States, except employees of Sears, Roebuck and Co., and the judges of this contest. Anyone may enter by submitting a complete patchwork quilt of his or her own making, which has never been previously exhibited.

•2•

All entries must be filled, backed, and quilted complete. No unquilted tops will be accepted. Quilts must be of adequate size to fit either a standard single or double bed.

•3•

Only one quilt can be entered by each contestant.

•4•

All quilts submitted will remain the property of the contestants except the Grand Prize Winner, which will be honored as noted elsewhere.

•5•

All quilts must be mailed (insured parcel post), addressed to your nearest Sears, Roebuck and Co. mail order house, or delivered to the Sears Retail Store on or before May 15, 1933.

•6•

Every possible care will be taken of the quilts, but Sears, Roebuck and Co. can assume no responsibility for fire, theft, or other agencies beyond its control.

•7•

No quilt can be entered in competition unless the official tag is securely sewed to the edge of the quilt in the lower right hand corner, completely filled out and signed. The official tag is enclosed or may be obtained at any Sears Retail Store participating in this Contest.

•8•

Prize-winning designs (designs only, not quilts) if original, will become the property of Sears, Roebuck and Co.

•9•

All quilts will be judged by impartial judges on a point basis,

SEARS, ROEBUCK AN

142. Interior pages of Sears contest entry brochure. Collection of Charles Fitzgerald and Margaret McDonald.

A CENTURY PLUS

The Contest's Aftermath

Following the 1933 fair, Sears, Roebuck and Company returned the exhibit quilts to their owners and presented the grand prize-winning quilt to Mrs. Eleanor Roosevelt. In the summer of 1934, A Century of Progress Exposition was reopened with repainted pavilions, more attractions, and new exhibits. At first, Sears chose not to reinstall the quilt exhibit since the company had plans for an exhibit of photographs of babies entered in the Sears National Baby Beauty Contest.

The baby contest attracted over 114,000 photographs. After local and state contests, photographs of the forty-nine finalists (one from each state and Alaska) were shown at the Sears Pavilion in the summer of 1934. For two months, visitors to the exhibit voted for the most beautiful baby, with the one receiving the highest number of votes being awarded $5,000 in cash and an educational policy of $5,000.[1]

Several weeks after the fair's 1934 opening, Sue Roberts, the Sears, Roebuck and Company home advisor and organizer of the 1933 quilt contest, bemoaned the fact that Sears had not planned a repeat of the highly successful quilt exhibit. In a July 27, 1934, letter to William R. Dunton, she wrote:

> Mr. Sears and Roebuck have temporarily lost their enthusiasm for [quilts] and have turned to babies instead. . . . We have had just a deluge of inquiries about a quilt display this year. It seems that any number of visitors came up primarily to see such an exhibit, having heard so much about the one last year. So great has

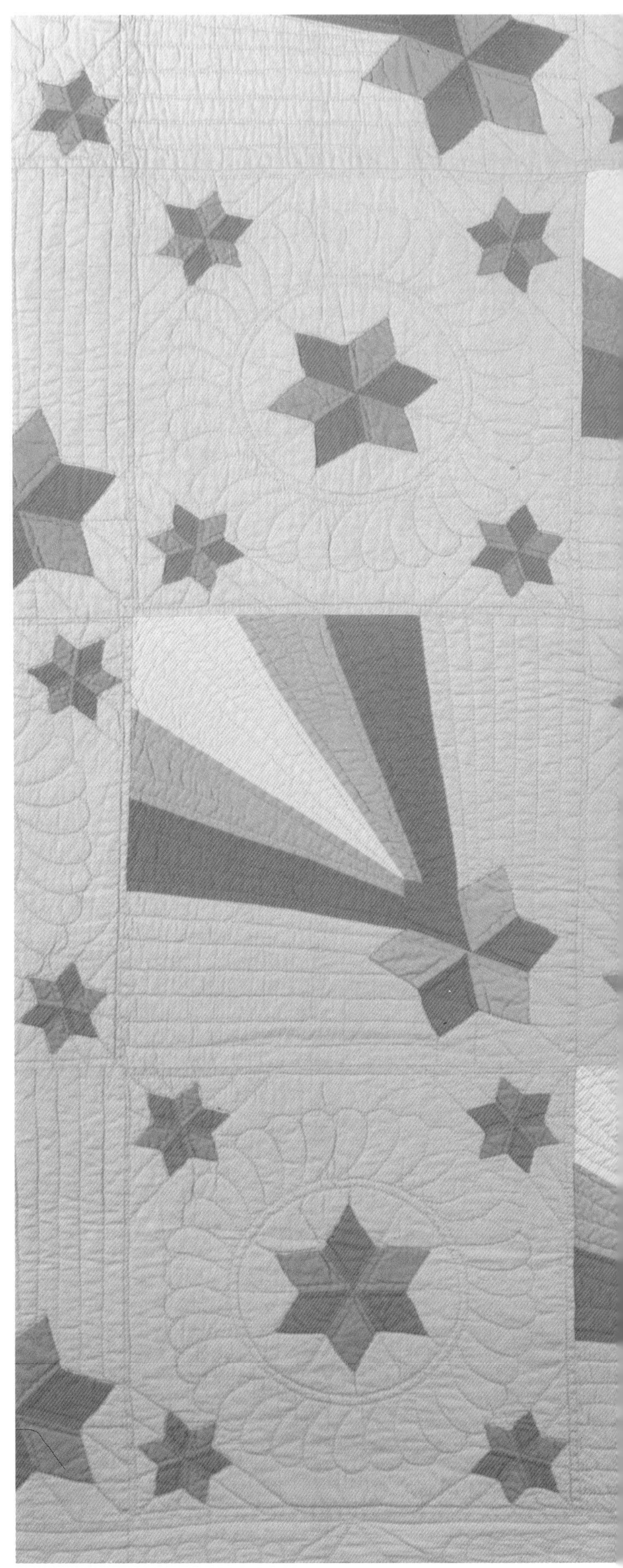

143. Detail of Star Arcturus (number 156, page 103)

been their disappointment that we are endeavoring to collect the first regional winners in an effort to give them something in that line, but I don't know how successful we will be. Of course, the grand prize-winner is in the White House, and we cannot very well ask for its loan. If it hadn't been for the huge amount of detail involved and the trouble of returning the thousands and thousands of rejected ones, I almost wish we had sponsored another contest.[2]

In response, William Dunton wrote, "It is of interest that you are having to get together another quilt show, and perhaps Sears, Roebuck will conclude there is something more to them than the sale of material, but I doubt it."[3]

On September 11, 1934, Roberts once again wrote to Dunton with a report on the success of the reinstalled quilt exhibit:

> Well, to talk of quilts for a moment, we were so overwhelmed with inquiries for them that we succumbed finally and called in the first regional prize-winners. Actually, the exhibit wasn't half in place before the people began flocking in from all parts of the grounds, just as birds wing their way over long stretches to a cooling pond or a fountain on a hot day. It doesn't seem possible that word could have traveled by mouth so quickly. The result is that we again have about the most popular spot at the fair.[4]

144. Reprint of the Sears baby contest brochure

145. Inez Ward of Horse Cave, Kentucky, won first prize in the Memphis regional contest with her Lincoln Quilt.

Inez Ward, the first place winner in the Memphis regional contest, reported in an interview that she thought a long time about returning her Lincoln quilt to the 1934 exhibit. "It took a beating [in the summer of 1933], even though it had cellophane over it. People had soiled it with their hands, especially down where my name was. But I told the people from the fair that they could have it back since they had been so nice."[5]

Edith Matthews saved a letter from Sue Roberts thanking her for participating in the second quilt display. At Christmas she received a large walnut sewing cabinet from Sears.

> November 20, 1934
>
> Dear Mrs. Matthews:
>
> We cannot begin to express our gratitude for the splendid way you came to our assistance and so willingly cooperated in making our second quilt display a success by lending us your beautiful prize winning quilt. Without a doubt, the exhibit was one of the most sought out spots in our entire building and ranked with the other outstanding attractions at the Fair.
>
> Within a few days you will receive a small token of this appreciation. It goes to you with our thanks and sincerest good wishes. We hope that it will serve as a pleasant reminder of a very happy association. Your quilt has already been returned by insured parcel post and should have reached you by this time.
>
> Again thanking you for responding so generously to our call and with kindest personal regards, we are
>
> Cordially yours,
>
> SEARS, ROEBUCK AND CO.
> Sue Roberts
> Home Advisor[6]

As Miss Roberts had indicated in her letters to William Dunton, Sears's objective in sponsoring a contest as a

146. Regional first prize winners on display at the 1934 Century of Progress Exposition *(left to right):* Lincoln Quilt by Inez Ward, Horse Cave, Kentucky; Stars by Rose White, Clarkston, Washington; Sunburst by Lillie Belle Carpenter, Hyndman, Pennsylvania; Unknown, probably made by Mrs. M. A. Harvey, Springfield, Massachusetts; Spectrum by Edith Matthews, Winnemuca, Nevada; Colonial Rose by Mabel Langley, Dallas, Texas; Autumn Leaves by Mary Hilliker, Carl Junction, Missouri; Star of France by Susie Combs, Pebworth, Kentucky; Tea Rose by Minnie Gau, Minneapolis, Minnesota.

marketing tool was a grand success. Other quilt supply houses also benefited from the publicity. Competitors jostled each other to appeal to quiltmakers eager to make exact duplicates of the prize winners.

Two pattern booklets were published featuring fair winners, and during the 1934 season, Sears sold its own pattern book. *Sears Century of Progress in Quilt Making* noted in the introduction that quilts once again had secured their place in the fine arts because of the quilt revival of the 1920s and 1930s, and they encouraged everyone to "MAKE A QUILT!!!"

The souvenir booklet had two purposes. The drawings would help the millions of visitors recall the "exquisite, perfect examples" of quiltmaking they had seen and they would inform those who "did not do the fair [about] the most famous and sought-after designs."[7]

147. Cover of *Sears Century of Progress in Quilt Making.*

The book included tips on quiltmaking, supplies available through the catalog and retail stores, and instructions for eleven of the prize-winning quilts with designs for matching pillows. A few of the original designs were simplified in the publication. The company gave no credit to the quiltmakers who had given up rights to their original designs by entering them in the Sears contest. However, the editors were careful to avoid printing any designs sold by other companies such as Home Art and Mountain Mist (See page 115 for names of uncredited quiltmakers and their patterns).

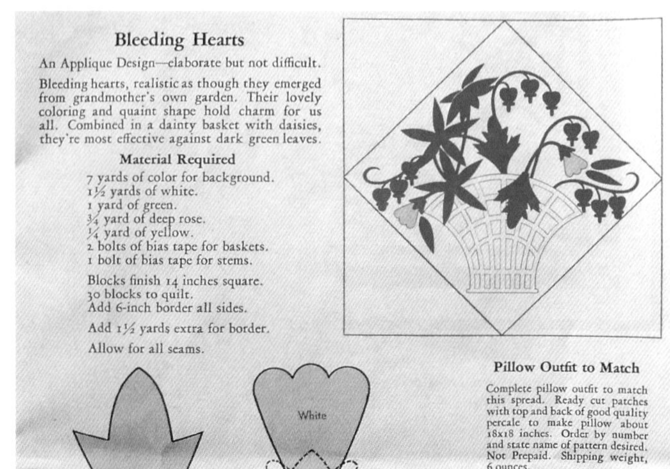

Bleeding Hearts

An Applique Design—elaborate but not difficult.

Bleeding hearts, realistic as though they emerged from grandmother's own garden. Their lovely coloring and quaint shape hold charm for us all. Combined in a dainty basket with daisies, they're most effective against dark green leaves.

Material Required

7 yards of color for background.
1½ yards of white.
1 yard of green.
¾ yard of deep rose.
¼ yard of yellow.
2 bolts of bias tape for baskets.
1 bolt of bias tape for stems.

Blocks finish 14 inches square.
30 blocks to quilt.
Add 6-inch border all sides.

Add 1½ yards extra for border.

Allow for all seams.

Pillow Outfit to Match

Complete pillow outfit to match this spread. Ready cut patches with top and back of good quality percale to make pillow about 18x18 inches. Order by number and state name of pattern desired. Not Prepaid. Shipping weight, 6 ounces.

149. Frances Klemenz's original design for her Bleeding Hearts quilt was modified by Sears for the pattern booklet *Sears Century of Progress in Quilt Making.*

148. Frances Klemenz, 1945

150. Detail of Bleeding Hearts

Frances Klemenz (1908–1987)

At the time of the contest, Frances Klemenz, a seamstress, had been unemployed for some time. She started work on her prize-winning quilt about February 15 and finished it a week before the deadline. She worked some days from 8:00 A.M. to 11:00 P.M. Her brother remembers going with the whole family to see the quilt on display at the fair. "We were very proud. As a family we shared the limelight."

Frances Klemenz also worked as a quilter for Regina, Inc., owned by Marguerite Kleinjohn of Louisville, and later as secretary to the vice president of Standard Oil of Louisville.

"I am overjoyed. I never dreamed I would win it, but I did put in many a long hour on it. I am too happy for words."—Frances Klemenz, when told by a news reporter of her first prize in the Louisville contest.

151. BLEEDING HEARTS

Maker: Frances Klemenz
Louisville, Kentucky, 1933

Appliquéd: 88″ x 69″; cotton

Frances Klemenz's quilt won third prize in the Chicago regional contest and was shown at the 1933 Chicago World's Fair.

Collection of Susan W. Smith, niece.

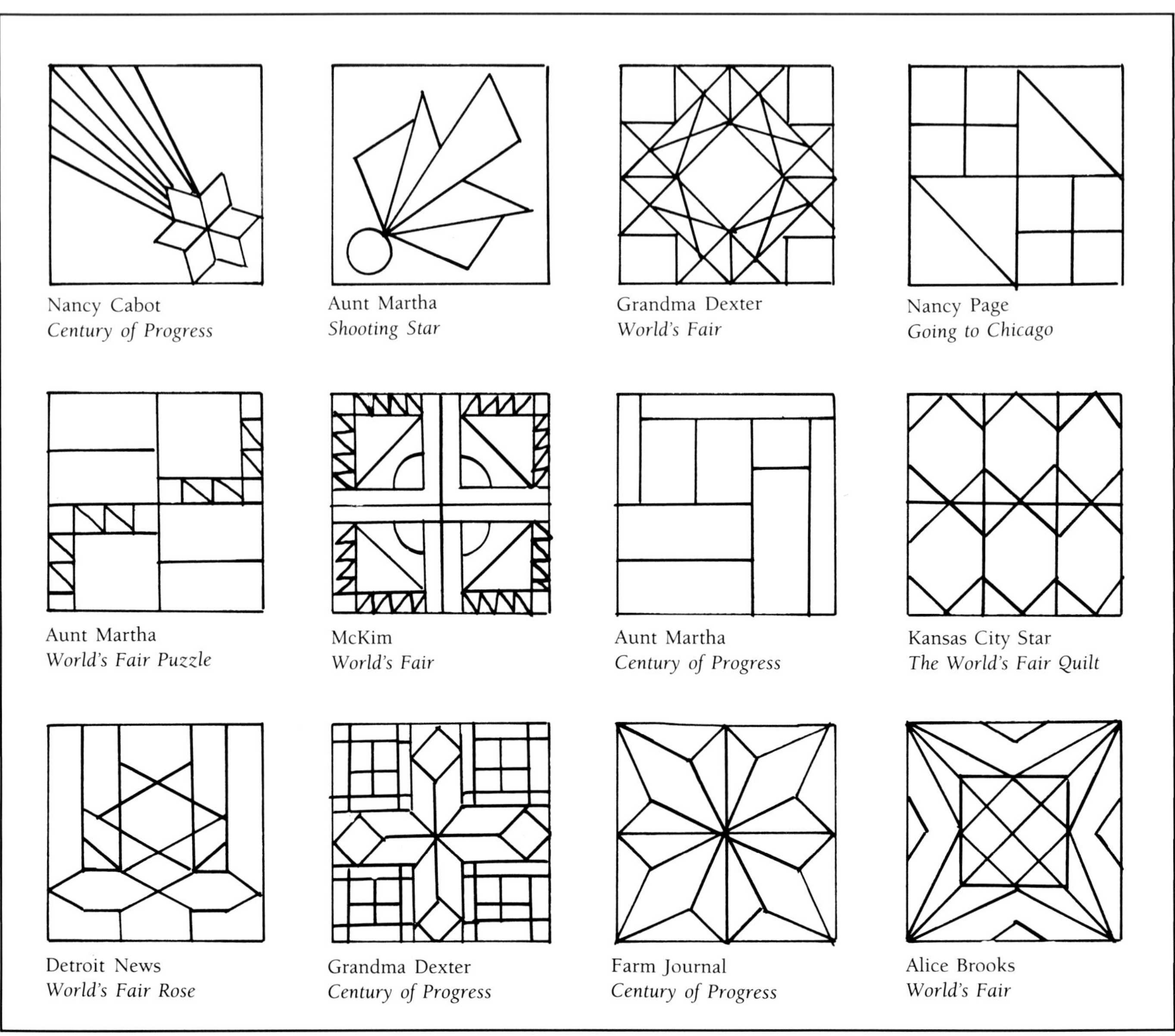

152. Commercial quilt blocks related to the 1933 Chicago World's Fair.

An "unofficial" pamphlet, "The Quilt Fair Comes to You," was offered by Aunt Martha's Studios through several national magazines. The twenty-five-cent booklet was advertised as a souvenir for those who had seen the exhibit and as an important record for those who had missed it. Among the one hundred patterns offered were several full-sized cutting patterns of fair entries and winners.

Quilt designers inspired by the fair offered original, commemorative patterns in their regular catalogs and syndicated columns. The Needlecraft Syndicate, which sold patterns under the names of Laura Wheeler and Alice Brooks, featured a World's Fair block in 1933 with the statement,

> The old-time patchwork quilt was an heirloom. It was not alone an economy; it was the needlewoman's interpretation of the things in her daily life and of the events of her time. Given such an occasion as the Fair at Chicago, she would have made a quilt to commemorate such an outstanding event. So, we today, following the spirit of the needlewoman of old, offer the World's Fair—a quilt, which in generations to come, will call to mind the remarkable exposition we now are having at Chicago. Like the designs of old, it too has meaning. Diversity of pattern—first you see one design, then it shifts to another—characterizes the variety of interests centered at the Exposition."[8]

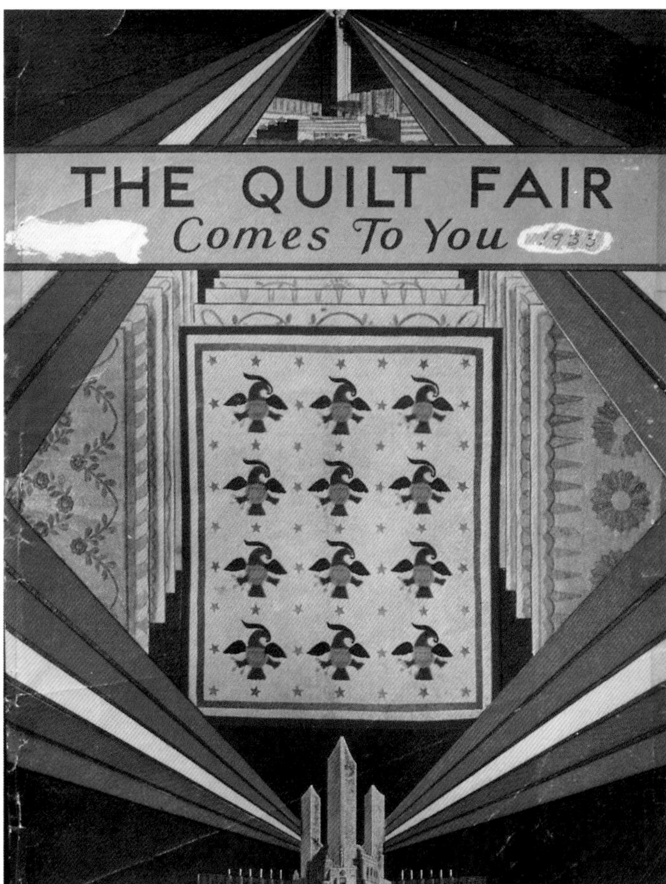

153. Cover of *The Quilt Fair Comes to You.* Collection of Merikay Waldvogel.

Quilting supply houses featured the winning quiltmakers in testimonials to their products. The Stearns and Foster Company, a Cincinnati batting manufacturer, asked prize winners about the cotton batting they had used. Edith Matthews, first prize winner in the Los Angeles regional contest, saved her letter from the company:

> October 14, 1933
>
> Dear Mrs. Matthews:
>
> Being much interested in quilts, several members of our company, who visited the World's Fair this Summer, were naturally delighted with the beauty of the prize-winning quilts in the Sears Roebuck exhibit. We have been manufacturing cotton batting for more than eighty years, and the recent revival in the quiltmaking art has encouraged us to improve our product to meet modern requirements.
>
> We wrote Miss Caden of Lexington, Ky., the winner of the Grand National Award, and were more than pleased to learn from her that her quilt was filled with our "White Rose" brand of cotton batting. This information was most pleasing, and has tempted us to write to the other winners to learn if they had used any one of our several brands of quilt fillings: Mountain Mist, White Rose, Pearl, Princess and Manchu.
>
> The Mountain Mist is the brand which we advertise and which we believe to be the most practical on the market, and to promote its sale, we publish and advertise the Mountain Mist quilt patterns. We ourselves have taken great pride in the fact that three of the thirty quilts exhibited in Chicago were of our design, namely, two quilts made from our Martha's Vineyard pattern and one quilt made from our New York Beauty pattern.
>
> Probably you have received much correspondence since you have received the award for your quilt, but if it is not asking too much, we would appreciate hearing from you as to the kind of filling you used in your quilt.
>
> Very truly yours,
>
> THE STEARNS & FOSTER CO.
> F. J. Hooker
> Sales Manager
> Putnam-Hooker Batting Dept.[9]

Georgia Litsey, second prize winner in the Memphis regional contest, was one of the two who used the Stearns and Foster Martha's Vineyard design. In the company's advertising, she praised the Mountain Mist patterns:

> I have used eight of them so far, and have taken prizes with four of them. My "Martha's Vineyard" was a Century of Progress prize winner in 1933. I know that these fine patterns were a marvelous help to me in securing prize-winning results.

(continued on page 104)

154. Mary Mihalovits Gasperik with her husband, Stephen, at Riverview Amusement Park in Chicago in the 1940s.

155. Detail of Star Arcturus

Mary Mihalovits Gasperik (1888–1969)

Born in a small village in Hungary in 1888, Mary received very little formal education but was taught to do fine needlework at home to help support the family. She emigrated to America with an older sister when she was sixteen and came to Chicago. In 1906 she married a fellow Hungarian, Stephen Gasperik, and they lived above and behind the grocery/meat market he owned on Chicago's South Side in an immigrant community.

She began making quilts about 1933 and embroidered the words "Century of Progress" on the back of several of her early examples. There is no evidence that she entered the Sears quilt contest, but she did enter quilts in Detroit in 1936–39 and won numerous awards for her beautifully appliquéd and quilted work.

Although she spoke limited English, she was active in the Tuley Park Quilt Club. Their appreciation of her fine work must have afforded her great pleasure and calm. Her granddaughter recalls Mary as somewhat tempestuous and quarrelsome, an energy which she translated into very beautiful, colorful, and creative quilts. Quilting became Mary Gasperik's main occupation, and by the time she died she had made nearly ninety quilts.

Information provided by Susan Krueger Salser and Karen Krueger Finn, granddaughters.

156. STAR ARCTURUS

Maker: Mary Mihalovits Gasperik
Chicago, Illinois, 1934

Pieced and appliquéd: 91″ x 77″; cotton

Collection of Susan Krueger Salser, granddaughter.

(continued from page 101)

She also advised all quiltmakers to use the Mountain Mist batting for "quilts that wash perfectly and have that evenly padded look that means so much to fine quilting."[10]

The Stiles Waxt Thread Company of Sycamore, Illinois, also used letters in its advertising that included a testimonial from Margaret Rogers Caden. Lillie Belle Carpenter inquired as to where she could purchase their thread and received this reply:

> November 24, 1933
>
> Dear Mrs. Carpenter:
> Stiles Waxt Thread retails at 15 cents a spool and the closest city to Hyndman which stocks our thread is Pittsburgh. . . . We had a note today from Miss Margaret Caden of Lexington, whose quilt "Star of the Blue Grass" won the $1,000 prize, and she tells us Stiles Waxt Thread was used on her quilt.
>
> Yours very truly,
>
> STILES WAXT THREAD COMPANY
> [Name illegible][11]

By awarding prizes to updated traditional quilts and by exhibiting them in public, Sears heightened the interest in quilts and quiltmaking. The exhibit, its ensuing publicity, and the published fair patterns broadened the audience of quilt enthusiasts. Whether people planned to make a quilt or have it made by a professional did not matter. Quilts had been elevated to the status of art. Thousands of traditional quiltmakers as well as quilt designers and professional quiltmakers were delighted.

157. Edith Morrow Matthews in front of her prize-winning quilt, The Spectrum, in 1933.

Edith Morrow Matthews (1885–1967)

Edith Morrow grew up in Geneseo, Illinois, the eldest of three sisters and three brothers. Her mother died at the birth of the youngest girl. As an adult Edith worked as a social worker and a homemaker. She married Ralph Matthews, a mechanical engineer, who helped her draft the design for The Spectrum when they lived in Winnemucca, Nevada. In the Sears contest, she won $210 in prizes for the original design. She used the money for living expenses since her husband had been ill and out of work for years. In Winnemucca she was known as the Bobcat Lady as she walked a pet bobcat on a leash. She left records of four later quilts. After the contest, the Matthewses moved to Wyoming, where Ralph died.

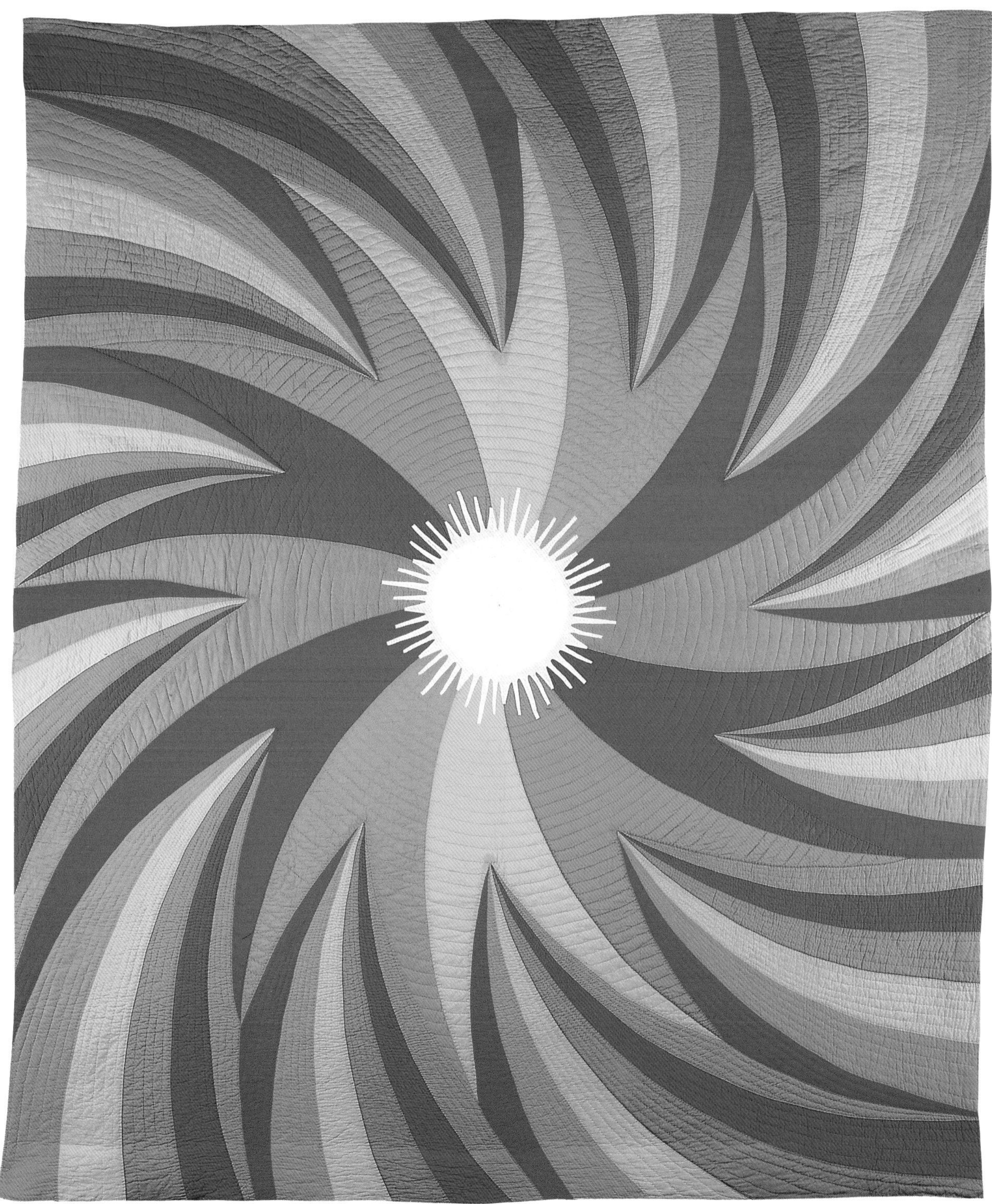

158. THE SPECTRUM

Maker: Edith Morrow Matthews
Winnemucca, Nevada, 1933

Pieced: 92″ x 76″; cotton

The quilt was judged best of 1,000 entries in the Los Angeles regional contest and displayed at the Century of Progress in both 1933 and 1934. A newspaper clipping described it as "quite gay and easy to find in its place of display."

Collection of Lucille and Phin Kinnaman, nephew.

"Take My Advice"... *says Mrs. George D. Litsey, Prominent Kentucky Quilt Authority...* "and Insist on MOUNTAIN MIST Quilting Cotton for Loveliest Quilting Results"

"I have been interested in quilts for years," writes Mrs. Litsey. "Ever since MOUNTAIN MIST Quilting Cotton came out, I have insisted on it for the filling of my quilts. I knew when I first heard of it that it would bring an amazing improvement over other types of quilt filling. Mrs. Blaine Wilson, of Travellers Rest, Kentucky, who does the actual quilting of my tops for me, tells me that this filling is a great deal easier to use; and I know from experience that my MOUNTAIN MIST filled quilts wash perfectly, and have that evenly padded look that means so much to fine quilting. ¶ "As for MOUNTAIN MIST Quilt Patterns, I'll just say this: I have used eight of them so far, and have taken prizes with four of them. My 'Martha's Vineyard' was a Century of Progress prize-winner in 1933. I know that these fine patterns were a marvelous help to me in securing prize-winning results."—*Mrs. George D. Litsey, Leitchfield, Kentucky.*

A FEW OUT OF HUNDREDS OF LETTERS WE HAVE RECEIVED

Space in this book forbids us to publish more than a few of the letters we have received. But these few sum up the sentiments in every one of hundreds of letters in our files:

"The more I use MOUNTAIN MIST, the better I like it. And the way it comes is a pleasure—all in one large sheet, which makes it so easy to work. I have made some beautiful quilts with the MOUNTAIN MIST Quilting Cotton and I am so glad I know about it. I wish every quilt maker would know of it, too. I tell everyone who asks me how I make such lovely quilts, that it's because I use the MOUNTAIN MIST; then I tell them all about it. I always have a roll or two on hand to show them how lovely and white it is."—Miss T. L. Haggerty, 461 Eighteenth St., Brooklyn, N. Y.

"We like the MOUNTAIN MIST Cotton very much. It is so smooth and so easy to handle and is such a nice large size. We still use it in all our quilting, for we insist on the best." Miss Laura Pickel, Route No. 1, Warnock, Ohio.

"Please send me the 'Dogwood' design No. 29. I know it will be a beauty. Have just finished the 'Dancing Daffodils,' and it is simply beautiful. You have the prettiest designs I ever saw, and I have quilted quite a few. Am a booster for MOUNTAIN MIST Cotton—it is so easy to quilt and quilting as many as I have, it takes something easy." Mrs. H. H. Nunn, Box 283, Groveland, Florida.

"Very often a customer asks me what type of filler she should purchase, and I unhesitatingly recommend MOUNTAIN MIST, for I know it assures a finer looking quilt, gives even puffing, will be easy to quilt, and washes beautifully." Mrs. Mary Wolter, 4836 N. Oakley Avenue, Chicago, Illinois.

159. Stearns and Foster Company advertisement with testimonial from Sears contest winner.

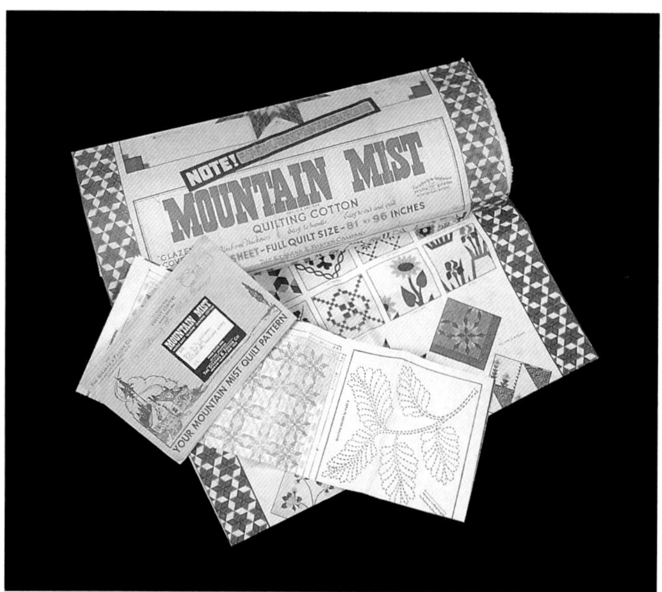

160. Mountain Mist batting with quilt patterns to order.

CONCLUSION

Patchwork is not the usual medium for recording history, but the quilts from the Century of Progress in Quiltmaking Contest have much to say about the Depression-era view of America's past and future. Many of the commemoratives are records of the 1933 World's Fair itself. The buildings on Lake Michigan are long gone, but the quilts tell us much about the Rainbow City and its fanciful visions of architecture's future.

The theme quilts also tell us about the concept of progress in the 1930s, themes that are now dated. The Euro-centric perspective of replacing "primitive" teepees with "civilized" temples is an old-fashioned idea. Today's appreciation of multicultural influences gives equal weight to the portable home of a Plains Native American and a temporary plaster exhibit hall. Equally dated is the glorified view of the future that quilters incorporated into their entries. The dirigible as the acme of progress in transportation is as out of date as the blind faith in technology as the savior of mankind.

The quilts also record the popular tastes of their times, letting us know the fabric, colors, and designs that appealed to women in the 1930s. In their stories the quilts reflect the grim seesaw of poverty and hope that so many rode in those years. In the tales of the winners we glimpse women's achievements in days when women were not permitted to achieve much outside their house work or fancy work. In the stories of the losers, we glimpse the dream castles that optimists build during hard times.

As we finish this book, we note that we have records of only 123 quilts entered in the Sears contest. Taking a lesson from the statisticians in Sears's public relations department, we calculate we are still looking for 24,755 quilts. We have also calculated that one in every two thousand American women entered the contest.[1] Does this mean we should find a World's Fair quilt in every American town with a population over 1,999? We admit we are skewing the data when we paint that rosy picture because the highest percentage have been found in the upper Midwest near Chicago. We hope, however, our statistical projection inspires readers to look around their own hometowns for the missing 24,755. Surely, many of these quilts are tucked away in linen closets, saved by families who have forgotten the story of Auntie's strange quilt, "the one with the comets."

If anyone finds Margaret Caden's Star of the Bluegrass quilt, please contact one of us immediately.

Correspondence may
be directed to:

Merikay Waldvogel
1501 Whitower Road
Knoxville, TN 37919

Barbara Brackman
500 Louisiana Avenue
Lawrence, KS 66044

The WINNERS. . .

in SEARS CENTURY of PROGRESS

QUILT CONTEST.

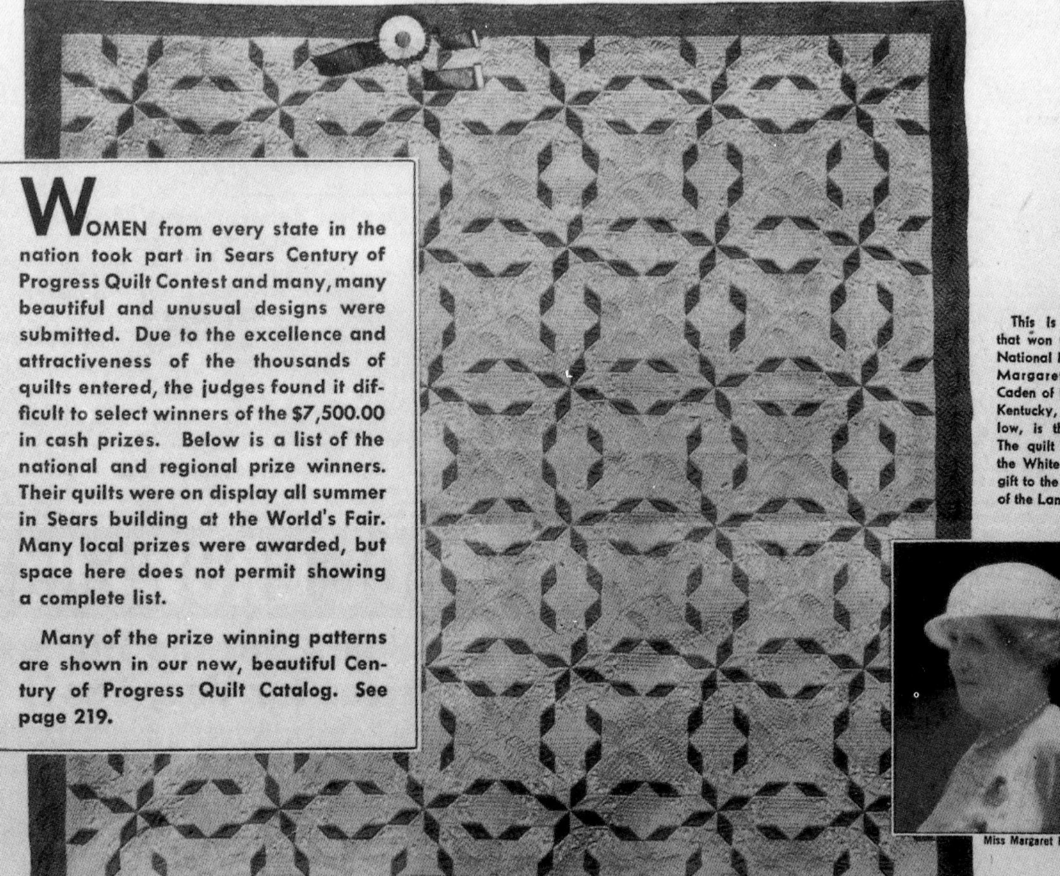

WOMEN from every state in the nation took part in Sears Century of Progress Quilt Contest and many, many beautiful and unusual designs were submitted. Due to the excellence and attractiveness of the thousands of quilts entered, the judges found it difficult to select winners of the $7,500.00 in cash prizes. Below is a list of the national and regional prize winners. Their quilts were on display all summer in Sears building at the World's Fair. Many local prizes were awarded, but space here does not permit showing a complete list.

Many of the prize winning patterns are shown in our new, beautiful Century of Progress Quilt Catalog. See page 219.

This is the quilt that won the Grand National Prize. Miss Margaret Rogers Caden of Lexington, Kentucky, shown below, is the winner. The quilt is now in the White House, a gift to the First Lady of the Land.

Miss Margaret Rogers Caden

National Prize Winners

1st Prize Miss Margaret Rogers Caden, Lexington, Kentucky

2nd Prize Miss Mabel Langley, Dallas, Texas

3rd Prize Miss Frieda V. Plume, Evanston, Illinois

Regional Prize Winners

ATLANTA
1st Prize: Mrs. Dale Combs, Pebworth, Ky.
2nd Prize: Mrs. Joe Wade, Knoxville, Tenn.
3rd Prize: Miss Martha Steele, Beattyville, Ky.

BOSTON
1st Prize: Mrs. M. A. Harvey, Springfield, Mass.
2nd Prize: Mrs. Grace M. Bentley, New Haven, Conn.
3rd Prize: Mrs. Mabel Hammond, Plattsburg, N. Y.

CHICAGO
1st Prize: Miss Margaret R. Caden, Lexington, Ky.
2nd Prize: Miss Frieda V. Plume, Evanston, Ill.
3rd Prize: Mrs. Frances Klemenz, Louisville, Ky.

DALLAS
1st Prize: Miss Mabel Langley, Dallas, Texas
2nd Prize: Mrs. Celia P. Hyde, Crowley, La.
3rd Prize: Miss Lois Hobgood, Iredell, Texas

KANSAS CITY
1st Prize: Miss Mary A. Hilliker, Carl Junction, Mo.
2nd Prize: Miss Emma Conry, Mascot, Nebr.
3rd Prize: Miss C. W. Veasy, Idaho Falls, Idaho

LOS ANGELES
1st Prize: Mrs. Ralph Matthews, Winnemucca, Nev.
2nd Prize: Miss Carrie B. Walker, Selma, Calif.
3rd Prize: Mrs. Rosetta Scott, Prescott, Ariz.

MEMPHIS
1st Prize: Mrs. Louis Ward, Horse Cave, Ky.
2nd Prize: Mrs. George Litsey, Leitchfield, Ky.
3rd Prize: Mrs. G. H. Wilkie, Shreveport, La.

MINNEAPOLIS
1st Prize: Miss Minnie Gau, Minneapolis, Minn.
2nd Prize: Mrs. Isabel Hughes, Linn Grove, Iowa
3rd Prize: Miss Rose Tekippe, Fort Atkinson, Iowa

PHILADELPHIA
1st Prize: Mrs. Virgil Carpenter, Hyndman, Pa.
2nd Prize: Mrs. G. R. Leitzel, Northumberland, Pa.
3rd Prize: Miss Edith Snyder, Buffalo, N. Y.

SEATTLE
1st Prize: Mrs. M. W. White, Clarkston, Wash.
2nd Prize: Mrs. W. E. Newton, Seattle, Wash.
3rd Prize: Mrs. S. J. Campbell, Freewater, Oregon

746 C101 Refer to INDEX for QUILT MAKING Supplies

161. Sears catalog page announcing the contest winners.

APPENDICES

Award Winners

SEARS NATIONAL QUILT CONTEST

Grand National Award

Margaret Rogers Caden
Route 3 Paris Pike
Lexington, Kentucky
$1,000 (includes Regional Prize)

Second National Award

Mabel Langley
3013 North Fitzhugh
Dallas, Texas
$500 (includes Regional Prize)

Third National Award

Frieda V. Plume
708 Dobson Street
Evanston, Illinois
$300 (includes Regional Prize)

Honorable Mention

Mrs. Dale Combs
Pebworth, Kentucky

Mary A. Hilliker
Carl Junction, Missouri

MINNEAPOLIS REGIONAL AWARDS

First Regional Award—$200

Minnie Gau
1455 Lagoon Avenue
Minneapolis, Minnesota

Second Regional Award—$75

Mrs. Isabel Hughes
Linn Grove, Iowa

Third Regional Winner—$25

Rose Tekippe
Fort Atkinson, Iowa

Mail Order Awards—$10 Each

Mrs. William Klinepier
Kasson, Minnesota

Mrs. Mate Palmer
Hawkeye, Iowa

Mrs. Isabel Hughes
Linn Grove, Iowa

Rose Tekippe
Fort Atkinson, Iowa

Mrs. G. D. Grosz
Ashley, North Dakota

Mail Order Awards—$5 Each

Junette Johnson
Wheaton, Minnesota

Mrs. Clate Haislet
West Concord, Minnesota

Mrs. Amanda Timm
Rapid City, South Dakota

Mrs. Wm. Frien (sp?)
Mt. Vernon, South Dakota

Mrs. Jane Baker
Dell, Montana

Florence Franklin
Rockford, Iowa

Mrs. Rosa Wells
Turner, Montana

Mrs. G. Cutler
Claremont, South Dakota

Ada Tekippe
Fort Atkinson, Iowa

Mrs. J. Luff (sp?)
Isanti, Minnesota

ATLANTA REGIONAL AWARDS

First Regional Award—$200

Mrs. Dale Combs
Pebworth, Kentucky

Second Regional Award—$75

Mrs. Joe Wade
Knoxville, Tennessee

Third Regional Awards—$25

Martha Steele
℅ R. L. Turner
Beattyville, Kentucky

Mail Order Awards—$10 Each

Grace Hiscock
Route 2, Box 97
Dixie, Georgia

Nora Griffith
South Fork, Kentucky

Mrs. Lynn Hoeflich
1009 Delaware Avenue
Fort Pierce, Florida

Mail Order Awards—$5 Each

Mrs. R. H. Edwards
Red Oak, North Carolina

Mattie McGuire
Pebworth, Kentucky

Bessie Bernard
Jamestown, Kentucky

Mrs. H. H. Walters
Route 6
Chattanooga, Tennessee

Mrs. John B. Darden
Route 2
LaFayette, Alabama

Mrs. M. C. Carr
Williamsburg, Kentucky

Mrs. Z. M. Abshear
Buckhorn, Kentucky

Edna Marie Brandenburg
Booneville, Kentucky

Florence Connor
17 Sixth Avenue
Andalusia, Alabama

Miss Lilly Noel
Madison Avenue
Athens, Tennessee

CHICAGO REGIONAL WINNERS

First Award—$200

Margaret Rogers Caden
Lexington, Kentucky

Second Award—$75

Frieda V. Plume
Evanston, Illinois

Third Award—$25

Frances Klemenz
Louisville, Kentucky

Mail Order House Awards

$10 each

Margaret Rogers Caden, Lexington, Kentucky
Mrs. R. E. Maack, Harvard, Illinois
Mrs. Orville Anderson, St. Jacob, Illinois
Dorothy Dwiggins, W. Alton, Missouri
Mrs. Ed. Dixon, Shelbyville, Illinois

$5 each

Emily Skelton, Toluca, Illinois
Essie E. Johnson, Pekin, Indiana
Mrs. Clyde Elliott, New Castle, Indiana
Mrs. J. M. Bridges, Elnora, Indiana
Mrs. Martin Schaida, Algoma, Wisconsin
Mrs. John McIntire, Brandenburg, Kentucky
Mrs. Doretta Hydorn, Bay City, Kentucky
Mrs. J. W. Taylor, Stamping Ground, Kentucky
Mildred Jacobs Chappell, Jerseyville, Illinois
Erma M. Walter, Carrollton, Illinois

MEMPHIS REGIONAL AWARDS

First Regional Award

Mrs. Louis Ward
Route 1
Horse Cave, Kentucky

Second Regional Award

Mrs. George D. Litsey
Leitchfield, Kentucky

Third Regional Award

Mrs. G. H. Wilkie
225 Wall Street
Shreveport, Louisiana

Mail Order House Awards

$5 each

Mrs. Louis Ward
Route 1
Horse Cave, Kentucky

Miss Orene Phillips
Route 1, Box 8
Savage, Mississippi

Miss Mary E. Carper
Prairie View, Arkansas

Mrs. D. D. Wilkins
Duck Hill, Mississippi

Mrs. Addie McCall
Huntingdon, Tennessee

$10 each

Mrs. George D. Litsey
Leitchfield, Kentucky

Mrs. G. H. Wilkie
225 Wall Street
Shreveport, Louisiana

Mrs. C. N. Chaney
Woodburn, Kentucky

Bertha Wethington
Pellyton, Kentucky

Mrs. W. C. Tyler
Duck Hill, Mississippi

Mrs. J. G. Woodruff
Woodburn, Kentucky

Miss Dixie Miller
669 University P., #3
Memphis, Tennessee

Mrs. C. H. Ross
Dukedom, Tennessee

Mrs. E. E. Wilkins
Duck Hill, Mississippi

Mrs. Fowler J. Crain
Route 1, Box 11
Munfordville, Kentucky

PHILADELPHIA REGIONAL AND MAIL ORDER AWARD WINNERS

Regional Award

1st Regional —$200 Mrs. Virgil W. Carpenter, Hyndman, Pennsylvania
2nd Regional— 75 Mrs. G. R. Leitzel, Northumberland, Pennsylvania
3rd Regional— 25 Mrs. Edith Snyder, Buffalo, New York

Mail Order Awards

$10 each

Mrs. H. Gorby, Littleton, West Virginia
Mrs. G. R. Leitzel, Northumberland, Pennsylvania
Mrs. Virgil W. Carpenter, Hyndman, Pennsylvania
Mrs. Chas. Houpt, East Liberty, Pennsylvania
Mrs. H. Kholer, Newfield, New Jersey

$5 each

Mrs. Ora E. Lowther, Berea, West Virginia
Mrs. J. A. McLaughlin, Marlinton, West Virginia
Hylda Corinne Mentzer, Altoona, Pennsylvania
Mrs. George Kanupkie, Ringtown, Pennsylvania
Mrs. Ella E. Garber, Timberville, Virginia
Mrs. Martha M. Spencer, Forestville, New York
Mrs. Emma J. Keefer, Millersburg, Pennsylvania
Mrs. Dorothy Evans Yurko, Hollidays Cove, West Virginia
Mrs. Floyd Poleman, Grantsville, Maryland
Mrs. Walter Hoffer, Jersey Shore, Pennsylvania

LOS ANGELES REGIONAL AWARDS

First Award—$200

Mrs. Ralph M. Matthews
71 Bell Street
Winnemucca, Nevada

Second Award—$75

Mrs. Carrie B. Walker
1635 Nebraska Avenue
Selma, California

Third Award—$25

Mrs. Rosetta Scott
641 Lincoln Avenue
Prescott, Arizona

NASHVILLE AWARD WINNERS

First Award

Miss Ruth Burrows
1306 Shelby Avenue
Nashville, Tennessee

Second Prize

Mrs. John DeWitt
1812 15th Avenue South
Nashville, Tennessee

Third Prize

Miss Roslyn Harrison
1800 8th Avenue South
Nashville, Tennessee

Honorable Mention

Mrs. Arthur A. Adams, Sr.
Birmingham, Alabama

Miss Beverly Orchard
Nashville, Tennessee

Mrs. Rufus Crowder
Lawrenceburg, Tennessee

Mrs. J. C. Pullum
Silver Point, Tennessee

Mrs. May Shrader
Nashville, Tennessee

Miss Florence Morrow
Franklin, Tennessee

Mr. Frenchy Cottrell
Nashville, Tennessee

Mrs. A. G. Maxwell
Cookeville, Tennessee

Mrs. H. H. Southern
Gallatin, Tennessee

Mrs. A. M. Russell
Rocky Mount, Tennessee

Mrs. N. L. Williams
McEwen, Tennessee

Mrs. George Stroud
McMinnville, Tennessee

Mrs. Walker Wilkins
Hopkinsville, Kentucky

Mrs. Robert Jennings
Nashville, Tennessee

LOUISVILLE AWARD WINNERS

First Award

Frances Klemenz
Louisville, Kentucky

Second Award

Mrs. Ova Gray
Louisville, Kentucky

Third Award

Mrs. S. H. McGill
Hogenville, Kentucky

Honorable Mention

Helen Schmidt
Sellersburg, Indiana

Daisy Shehan
Valley Station, Kentucky

Mrs. C. Deuser
Louisville, Kentucky

Mrs. W. D. Simmons
Ekron, Kentucky

Mrs. Essie McCoy
Louisville, Kentucky

Mrs. Flora Conner
New Albany, Indiana

Mrs. P. Graham
Louisville, Kentucky

Mrs. John Shouse
Lexington, Kentucky

Mrs. E. R. Bagby
Bowling Green, Kentucky

List of Quilts Entered or Inspired by 1933 Sears National Quilt Contest in Alphabetical Order by Maker's Name

Maker's Name	Made In	Title
Anonymous		State Flower Qlt
Anonymous		Century of Progress
Anonymous		Peacock
Anonymous		Album of Inventors
Anonymous		Dogwood Appliqué
Anonymous		I Will Quilt
Anonymous		Clipper Ship
Anonymous		Star of Bluegrass
Anonymous		Star w/ Chgo Skyline
Anonymous		1833–1933 & Arcturus
Anonymous		Clipper Ship on Sea
Anonymous		Y in Center
Anonymous		Teepees to Temples
Anonymous		Sears Bldg 1833–1933
Anonymous		Historic Scenes
Anonymous		Chicago Fire
Anonymous		Lg Bldg w/teepee
Anonymous		Arcturus Star
Anonymous		Sears Bldg w/ Eagles
Anonymous		Map of USA
Anonymous		Century of Progress
Anonymous		Roosevelt Qlt
Anonymous		Century Plant
Anonymous	IL	Whig Rose Appliqué
Anonymous		Commemorative—Gene Autry Museum
Adams, Elizabeth	IL	Chicago Fireworks
Andres, Emma	AZ	Lady at the Spinning Wheel
Backfish, Olive	IN	Century of Progress
Baker, Antonnette	IL	Crazy Quilt
Barnfield, Mayme	IL	Garden Kaleidoscopes
Baxter, Florence	IL	Flower Garden
Bentley, Grace	CT	
Betourne, Antoinette	IL	Iris
Bitter, Louella	IL	Floridian Gardens
Bradley, Mary E.	OH	
Caden, Margaret	KY	Unknown Star
Carpenter, Mrs. Virgil	PA	Sunburst
Chappell, Mildred	IL	Commemorative
Christophal, Martha	IL	Comm. with Peacock
Clemens, Beulah	WA	Sunflower
Collord, Myrtle	ID	Map of World
Combs, Mrs. Dale	KY	Star of France
Crowell, Lois	TX	Bowl of Flowers
Cummings, Alma	IA	Vases of Flowers
DeWitt, Rebekah Ward	TN	Lily of the Valley
Dubray, Katherine	MO	Baby-Whole Cloth
Dyer, Aurora	IL	Century of Progress
E. H.	OH	Bow with Bouquet
Fitzgerald, Elizabeth	NY	Transportation Qlt
Fitzgerald, Mary	IL	Fort Dearborn
Ford, Renae		
Freeman, Mrs. I. J.	IL	Floral Appliqué
Galbraith, Etelka	IL	May Garden
Gasperik, Mary	IL	Floral Vine
Gasperik, Mary	IL	Appliqué Tulip
Gasperik, Mary	IL	Nancy Cabot Star
Girvin, Mary Stone	IL	Colonial Rose
Hall, Matilda		Floral Wreath Appliqué
Hansen, Anna	IL	Century of Progress
Hastings, Mattie	KY	Flower Girl
Hilliker, Mary	MO	Autumn Leaves
Hughes, Isabell	IA	Delectable Mountains
Hunter, Eva	IL	Mariner's Compass
Hyde, Celia	LA	Louisiana Rose
Johnson, Thelma Burleigh	MN	Scenes of Early Amer
Kanupkie, Cora	PA	Sunrise
Kendall, Chestine		Commemorative
Klemenz, Frances	KY	Bleeding Hearts
Kolling, Johanna	IL	New York Beauty
Lambrecht, Alfred	TX	Tulip Pattern
Langley, Mabel	TX	Colonial Rose
Lathouse, Effie	OH	Century of Progress
Lathouse, Effie	OH	History of Transportation
Leaton, Effie	IL	Teepees to Temples
Leitzel, Mrs. G. R.	PA	Commemorative
Leonhard, Emma	IL	1833 to 1933
Light, Ruth	IN	Commemorative
Litsey, Georgia	KY	Martha's Vineyard
Longsworth, Jeanette	OH	1933
Mandish, Rita		Pieced Tulip
Matthews, Edith	NV	Spectrum
McDaniel, Irene	MO	Commemorative
Montgomery, Lora	IN	Century of Progress
Morse, Permilia	KS	Broken Star
Mounts, Mrs. W. L.	IL	Magpie Rose
Mueller, Marie	IA	Cornucopia
Nolte, Minnie Tappe	WV	Double Wedding Ring
Normann, Fanny & Charles	TX	Century of Progress
Pederson, Florence	WI	Commemorative
Phelan, Mrs. J. R.	OK	Oklahoma History Qlt
Plowman, Ella	IL	New York Beauty
Plume, Frida	IL	Delectable Mountains
Poetz, Marie	MI	Century of Progress

Maker's Name	Made In	Title
Porter, Lelia	AL	Crown of Thorns
Prebbel, Sarah	IL	Fort Dearborn
Price, Georgiana		Meet Me at the Fair
Raddatz, Ruby	WA	Work and Play
Rebenstorff, Linda	WI	Century of Progress
Ringhoffer, Henrietta	TX	State Flower Quilt
Rowley, Louise	IL	Fair Site from Air
Schmidt, Erma	WI	Yo Yo Quilt
Simon, Edith	IL	State Flower Quilt
Skillestad, Grace	MT	All American Star
Stahlschmidt, Dorothy	IL	Lone Star
Steele, Martha	KY	
Stenge, Bertha	IL	Chicago Fair
Stewart, Virgie	IL	Dogwood Appliqué
Tekippe, Rose	IA	New York Beauty
Teska, Mary	MI	Couples of Many Nations
Tripp, B. & Mary Blee	IL	Fan
Underwood, Alice	IN	Star of Arcturus
Vasey, I. & M. Wasser	MI	Garden Bouquet
Wade, Florence	TN	Iris
Ward, Inez	KY	Lincoln Quilt
Wetzel, Olive	IL	State of Illinois
White, Rose	WA	Blazing Star-Commemorative
Wilkie, Mrs. C. H.	LA	
Wise, Samantha Allison	TN	Century of Progress

Additional Quilts Located Since First Printing

Maker's Name	Made In	Title
Anonymous		Stripes and Stars
Fordyce, Lillian	PA	Calendar Quilt
Giroux, Hermina	VT	Century of Progress
Hammond, Mabel	NY	Dresden Plate
Harrington, Theodora	PA	Century of Progress
Halgeson, Allena	MN	Roosevelt Quilt
Kentucky Quilters	KY	Caden Duplicate
Schoeffler, Mrs. Frank	ND	Zodiac Signs

Quiltmakers of unattributed quilts in *Sears Century of Progress in Quilt Making*

An original design by Emma Conry of Mascot, Nebraska; Bleeding Hearts by Frances Klemenz of Louisville, Kentucky; Tea Rose by Minnie Gau of Minneapolis, Minnesota; Bowl of Flowers by Lois Hobgood, Iredell, Texas; Autumn Leaves by Mary Hilliker of Carl Junction, Missouri, and Edith Snyder of Buffalo, New York; Louisiana Rose by Celia Hyde of Crowley, Louisiana; Delectable Mountains by Frida V. Plume of Evanston, Illinois; Martha's Vineyard by Georgia Litsey of Leitchfield, Kentucky; Colonial Rose by Mabel Langley of Dallas, Texas; and Iris by Florence Wade of Knoxville, Tennessee.

ORIGINS OF ILLUSTRATED QUILTS

Alabama

Crown of Thorns

Arizona

Lady at the Spinning Wheel

Illinois

Century of Progress
Century of Progress
Century of Progress/World Without End
Chicago Fair
1833 to 1933
Floridian Garden
Fort Dearborn
Garden Kaleidoscopes
Magpie Rose
May Garden
Star of Arcturus
State of Illinois

Indiana

Sears Pavilion

Iowa

Vases of Flowers
New York Beauty
Cornucopia

Kentucky

Bleeding Hearts

Louisiana

Louisiana Rose

Minnesota

Scenes from Early America

Nevada

The Spectrum

New York

Transportation Quilt

Ohio

Nineteen Hundred Thirty Three

Pennsylvania

Sunburst

Tennessee

Iris

Texas

Bowl of Flowers
Historic USA

Wisconsin

Rebenstorff Quilt

Unknown

Album of Inventors
Century of Progress
Clipper Ship
I Will Quilt
Star of the Bluegrass

Notes

Preface

1. See Sears Contest articles by Barbara Brackman, Cuesta Benberry, and Joyce Gross in *Quilters' Journal* 27 (July 1985); Barbara Brackman, "Looking Back at the Great Quilt Contest," *Quilter's Newsletter Magazine* 156 (October 1983): 22–24.

The Rainbow City: Chicago and the Fair

1. James O'Donnell Bennett, "Chicago Dubbed 'Windy' in Fight for Fair of '93," *Chicago Tribune,* June 11, 1933, part 1, p. 8, col. 1.
2. *Chicago Souvenir Guide to the Century of Progress* (Chicago: The Fair Guide Publishers, 1932).
3. Cathy Cahan and Richard Cahan, "The Lost City of the Depression," *Chicago History* 5 (1976–77): 237.
4. Lenox R. Lohr, *Fair Management: The Story of a Century of Progress Exposition* (Chicago: The Cuneo Press, 1952): 63.
5. *Ibid.,* 9.
6. *Ibid.,* 267.
7. *Ibid.,* 30–31.
8. Rufus Dawes, "Dawes Pictures Benefits from the Exposition," *Chicago Herald Examiner,* May 14, 1931.
9. Barbara Haggard Matteson, "Yesterday's City," *Chicago History* (Fall 1983): 68–69.
10. *Ibid.,* 69.
11. Cahan, 235.
12. *Ibid.,* 234.
13. *Ibid.,* 235.
14. "America Keen to Get New Ideas and Inspiration," *New York Times Magazine,* August 5, 1934, p. 5.
15. "514,514 Persons Pay to View World's Fair," *Atlanta Constitution,* June 4, 1933.
16. *Official Guide of the Fair, 1933* (Chicago: A Century of Progress, 1934).
17. "Beam of Light from Distant Star Will Throw Switch, Opening Chicago's Fair," *Lexington Leader,* May 26, 1933, p. 1.
18. *World's Fair Weekly,* June 18, 1933, p. 57.
19. Lohr, 73.
20. *Ibid.,* 75.
21. *Ibid.,* 106.
22. *Ibid.,* 126.
23. *Ibid.,* 233–234.
24. *Ibid.,* 72.
25. *Ibid.,* 200.
26. *Ibid.,* 172.
27. Stanley Gwynn, "Yesterday's City," *Chicago History* (Fall 1983): 70.
28. "Sears Building—Nashville World's Fair Headquarters," *Nashville Banner,* May 25, 1933.
29. "Where All the World Can Rest," *World's Fair Daily,* 24–25, in A Century of Progress Files in the collection of the University Library at the University of Illinois, Chicago Circle.
30. Lohr, 253.
31. Studs Terkel, *Hard Times* (New York: Avon Books, 1971): 204.

A Century of Progress in Quiltmaking: The Quilting Contest

1. A. P. Tarver, "Grandmother's Quilts," *Southern Agriculturalist,* June 1928.
2. Stearns and Foster Company, clipping from a booklet possibly entitled *The Romance of the Quilt* (Cincinnati: Stearns and Foster Company, 1934).
3. Circular, "Sears Century of Progress Quilt Contest," in collection of H. M. Carpenter.

America's Champion Quilter: The Contest and the Prize

1. J. H. White, letter to Ross Bartley, October 12, 1932. A Century of Progress, Special Collections, University of Illinois at Chicago Circle Library.
2. Letter from Bartley to White, November 14, 1932. A Century of Progress, Special Collections, University of Illinois at Chicago Circle Library.
3. "Sears Century of Progress Quilt Contest," n.d.
4. Sears, Roebuck and Company, catalog no. 166 (1933): 126.
5. Marie Mueller, letter to Barbara Brackman, June 9, 1982.
6. Lois Hobgood Crowell, telephone interview with Barbara Brackman, November 20, 1982.
7. H. Ver Mehren, *Colonial Quilts* (Des Moines: Home Arts, 1933), 6.
8. L. W. Thompson, letter to Mrs. Virgil Carpenter, June 12,

1933. Mrs. Virgil Carpenter, letter to L. W. Thompson, June 17, 1933.

9. Ida M. Stow, letter to Sears, Roebuck and Company, June 6, 1933, quoted in *Quilters' Journal* (July 1985): 13.

10. Sue Roberts, letter to William Rush Dunton, Jr., May 9, 1934. The William Rush Dunton, Jr., Papers. The Baltimore Museum of Art.

11. Mueller, letter.

12. Sue Roberts, letter to William Rush Dunton, Jr., May 9, 1934. The William Rush Dunton, Jr., Papers. The Baltimore Museum of Art.

13. Louise Fowler Roote, "This Quilt Won the Thousand Dollar Prize," *Capper's Weekly* (May 26, 1934).

14. "Check for $1,000, Representing First Prize in Sears National Quilting Contest, Is Presented to Miss Caden," *Lexington Herald Leader,* June 18, 1933.

15. Margaret Caden, letter to Mrs. Virgil Carpenter, July 5, 1933. Note that the meaning of the word *gingham* has changed over the past fifty years. Today's gingham means a checked fabric; in the past gingham meant fine woven plain cotton.

16. Much of the information about the true story of the prize-winning quilt was obtained through interviews with family members. The authors interviewed Helen Black, October 4, 1984, and February 11, 1992; Elberta Botner, February 9, 1992; Sarah Caden, February 11, 1992; Louise Eddleman, June 27, 1989, and February 9, 1992; Ruth Stewart, February 10, 1992; and Bess Brandenburg, August 12, 1992.

17. Louise Eddleman, telephone interview with Robert Cogswell, September 24, 1989, quoted in Waldvogel, *Soft Covers for Hard Times* (Nashville: Rutledge Hill Press, 1990): xii–xiii.

18. The Home Department, Eastern States Exposition (Storrowton, Massachusetts), 1936.

19. Dorothy West, interviewed with the Federal Writers Project, New York, 1938, in Ann Banks, ed., *First Person America* (New York: A. A. Knopf, 1980): 11.

20. Cuesta Benberry, "Quilt Cottage Industries: A Chronicle," *Uncoverings 1986* (San Francisco: American Quilt Study Group, 1987): 88.

21. Botner, interview.

22. Reva Crabtree, interview with authors, February 10, 1992.

23. Clara Belle Thompson and Margaret Lukes Wise, "Quilts That Went to the County Fair," *Country Gentleman* 62 (November 1992): 80.

24. Bertha Hensley, interview with authors, February 10, 1992.

From Teepees to Temples: The Commemorative Quilts

1. Leon Harpole, letter to A. H. Kirkland, June 12, 1933. A Century of Progress, Special Collections, University of Illinois at Chicago Circle Library.

2. Nancy Cabot, "Star Arcturus Sheds Its Light on Century of Progress Quilt," *Chicago Tribune,* October 22, 1933.

3. Letter from scrapbook of Lenice Ingram Bacon in Joyce Gross Collection.

4. Emma Mae Leonhard, "From 1833 to 1933—Explanation of the Meaning of the Quilt Blocks and Quilting Design," provided by quilt owner Ardis James.

A Century Plus: The Contest's Aftermath

1. Sears Century of Progress Baby Contest flier in the Century of Progress files at Special Collections Department, University Library, University of Illinois at Chicago.

2. Sue Roberts, letter to William Rush Dunton, Jr., July 27, 1934, The William Rush Dunton, Jr., Papers, The Baltimore Museum of Art.

3. William Rush Dunton, Jr., letter to Sue Roberts, August 1, 1934, The William Rush Dunton, Jr., Papers, The Baltimore Museum of Art.

4. Sue Roberts, letter Dr. William Rush Dunton, Jr., September 11, 1934, The William Rush Dunton, Jr., Papers, The Baltimore Museum of Art.

5. Barbara Brackman, "Looking Back at the Great Quilt Contest," *Quilter's Newsletter Magazine* 156 (October 1983): 22–24.

6. Sue Roberts, letter to Mrs. Ralph M. Matthews, November 20, 1934, in collection of Lucille and Phin Kinnaman.

7. *Sears Century of Progress in Quilt Making* (Chicago: Sears, Roebuck and Company, 1934).

8. Laura Wheeler, World's Fair pattern no. 507, in quilt pattern collection of Merikay Waldvogel.

9. F. J. Hooker, letter to Mrs. Ralph M. Matthews, October 14, 1933, in collection of Lucille and Phin Kinnaman.

10. Stearns and Foster Company advertisement, no date.

11. Stiles Waxt Thread Company, letter to Mrs. Virgil Carpenter, November 24, 1933, in collection of H. M. Carpenter.

Conclusion

1. We estimated this figure by taking the 1930 population of the United States (approximately 126,000,000), of which a little more than half were women (63,000,000), deducting approximately 20 percent who were too young to quilt, thus leaving 50,000,000 potential quiltmakers. Sears estimated they had 25,000 entries, or 1 from every 2,000 American women.

Bibliography

CHICAGO HISTORY AND ITS WORLD'S FAIRS

Burg, David F. *Chicago's White City of 1893*. Lexington: University of Kentucky Press, 1977.

Cahan, Cathy, and Richard Cahan. "The Lost City of the Depression." *Chicago History* 5, no. 4 (1976–77).

Condit, Carl W. *Chicago: 1930–70: Building, Planning, and Urban Technology*. Chicago: University of Chicago Press, 1974.

Design, 35, no. 4 (October 1933).

Design, 36, no. 2 (June 1934).

Gordon, Lois, and Alan Gordon. *American Chronicle: Six Decades in American Life 1920–1980*. New York: Macmillan Publishing Company, 1987.

Lohr, Lenox R. *Fair Management: The Story of A Century of Progress Exposition*. Chicago: The Cuneo Press, 1952.

Matteson, Barbara Haggard. "Yesterday's City." *Chicago History* (Fall 1893): 68–71.

Pierce, Bessie Louise. *A History of Chicago*. 3 vols. New York: A. A. Knopf, 1937.

Wagenknecht, Edward. *Chicago*. Norman: University of Oklahoma Press, 1964.

HISTORY OF SEARS, ROEBUCK AND COMPANY

Emmet, Boris, and John E. Jeuck. *Catalogues and Counters: A History of Sears, Roebuck and Company*. Chicago: University of Chicago Press, 1950.

Fairchild Publications. *The Story of Sears, Roebuck and Company*. New York: Fairchild Publications, 1961.

Katz, Donald R. *The Big Store: Inside the Crisis and Revolution at Sears*. New York: Viking, 1987.

Weil, Gordon. *Sears Roebuck, USA: The Great American Catalog Store and How It Grew*. Briarcliff Manor, New York: Stein and Day, 1977.

Worthy, James C. *Shaping an American Institution: Robert E. Wood and Sears, Roebuck*. Champaign: University of Illinois Press, 1984.

DEPRESSION ERA

Horan, James David. *The Desperate Years, A Pictorial History of the Thirties*. New York: Crown Publishers, 1962.

Hoge, Cecil C. *The First Hundred Years Are the Toughest*. Berkeley, California: Ten Speed Press, 1988.

Jenkins, Alan. *The Thirties*. Briarcliff Manor, New York: Stein and Day, 1976.

Manchester, William. *The Glory and the Dream: A Narrative History of America 1932–1972*.

Terkel, Studs. *Hard Times*. New York: Avon Books, 1971.

TWENTIETH CENTURY QUILT HISTORY

Atkins, Jacqueline M., and Phyllis A. Tepper. *New York Beauties: Quilts from the Empire State*. New York: Dutton Studio Books, 1992.

Benberry, Cuesta. "The Twentieth Century's First Quilt Revival." *Quilter's Newsletter Magazine,* 114 (July/August 1979): 20.

Brackman, Barbara. *Clues in the Calico: A Guide to Identifying and Dating Antique Quilts*. Alexandria, Virginia: EPM Publications, Inc., 1989.

———. *Encyclopedia of Pieced Quilt Patterns*. Paducah, Kentucky: American Quilters' Society, 1993.

———. "Virgie Stewart and the Tuley Park Quilting Club." *Quilter's Journal,* 31 (1987): 14–16.

Dunton, William Rush, Jr. *Old Quilts*. Cantonsville, Maryland: privately printed, 1946.

Finley, Ruth. *Old Patchwork Quilts and the Women Who Made Them*. Reprint. McLean, Virginia: EPM Publications, 1992.

Hall, Carrie A., and Rose G. Kretsinger. *The Romance of the Patchwork Quilt in America*. New York: Bonanza Books, 1935.

Horton, Laurel, ed. *Uncoverings*. San Francisco: American Quilt Study Group, 1980–1992.

Ickis, Marguerite. *The Standard Book of Quilt Making and Collecting*. 1949. Reprint. New York: Dover Publications, 1959.

Laury, Jean Ray, and California Heritage Quilt Project. *Ho for California!* New York: E. P. Dutton, 1990.

MacDowell, Marsha, and Ruth D. Fitzgerald, eds. *Michigan Quilts: 150 Years of a Textile Tradition*. East Lansing, Michigan: Michigan State University, 1987.

McKim, Ruby S. *101 Patchwork Patterns*. 2nd ed. New York: Dover Publications, 1962.

Nickols, Pat L. "Mary A. McElwain: Quilter and Quilt Businesswoman" in *Uncoverings 1991*. Edited by Laurel Horton. San Francisco: American Quilt Study Group, 1992.

Orlofsky, Myron, and Patsy Orlofsky. *Quilts in America*. New York: McGraw Hill, 1974.

Perry, Rosalind Webster, and Marty Frolli. *A Joy Forever: Marie Webster's Quilt Patterns*. Santa Barbara: Practical Patchwork, 1992.

Roote, Louise Fowler. *Kate's Blue Ribbon Quilts*. Topeka: Capper's Publishing, 1934.

Waldvogel, Merikay. "The Marketing of Anne Orr's Quilts" in *Uncoverings 1990*. Edited by Laurel Horton. San Francisco: American Quilt Study Group, 1991.

Webster, Marie. *Quilts: Their Story and How to Make Them*. Santa Barbara: Practical Patchwork, 1991.

Woodard, Thomas K., and Blanche Greenstein. *Twentieth Century Quilts 1900–1950*. New York: E. P. Dutton, 1988.

THE 1933 SEARS NATIONAL QUILT CONTEST

Benberry, Cuesta. "A Record of National Quilt Contests." *Quilter's Newsletter Magazine* 213 (June 1989): 28–30, 54.

Beyer, Alice. *Quilting*. Chicago: South Park Commissioners, 1934. Reprint. East Bay Heritage Quilters, 1978.

Brackman, Barbara. "Looking Back at the Great Quilt Contest." *Quilter's Newsletter Magazine* 156 (October 1973): 22–24.

———. "Patterns from the 1933 Chicago World's Fair." *Quilter's Newsletter Magazine,* 134 (July/August 1981): 18–23, 30–31.

———. "Quilts at Chicago's World's Fairs" in *Uncoverings 1981*. Edited by Sally Garouette. Mill Valley, California: American Quilt Study Group, 1982.

Gross, Joyce. *Quilters' Journal* 28 (December 1985).

The Quilt Fair Comes to You. Kansas City: Colonial Patterns, 1934.

Sears, Roebuck and Company. *A Century of Progress in Quilt Making*. Chicago, 1934.

Turner, Amy C. "Mom's World's Fair Quilt" in *Quilter's Newsletter Magazine,* 46 (August 1973): 24.

Waldvogel, Merikay. *Soft Covers for Hard Times: Quiltmaking and the Great Depression*. Nashville: Rutledge Hill Press, 1990.

INDEX

Boldface signifies quilts illustrated in the text.